Has Globalization Gone Far Enough?

The Costs of Fragmented Markets

Has Globalization Gone Far Enough?

The Costs of Fragmented Markets

Scott Bradford and Robert Z. Lawrence

Institute for International Economics
Washington, DC
February 2004

Scott C. Bradford is assistant professor at the department of economics, Brigham Young University. His research interests include international trade, political economy, and the Japanese economy. His work has appeared in *The American Economic Review*, *The Review of Economics and Statistics*, and the *Journal of International Economics*.

Robert Z. Lawrence, senior fellow, is also the Albert L. Williams Professor of Trade and Investment at the John F. Kennedy School of Government at Harvard University. He served as a member of President Clinton's Council of Economic Advisers from 1999 to 2000. He held the New Century Chair as a nonresident senior fellow at the Brookings Institution between 1997 and 1998 and founded and edited the *Brookings Trade Forum* in 1998. He is the author of several books, including *Crimes and Punishments? Retaliation under the WTO* (2003).

INSTITUTE FOR INTERNATIONAL ECONOMICS
1750 Massachusetts Avenue, NW
Washington, DC 20036-1903
(202) 328-9000   FAX: (202) 659-3225
www.iie.com

C. Fred Bergsten, *Director*
Valerie Norville, *Director of Publications and Web Development*

Typesetting by MidAtlantic Books & Journals, Inc.
Printing by United Book Press, Inc.
Cover photo: Don Bishop/Getty Images

Printed in the United States of America
06 05 04   5 4 3 2 1

Library of Congress Cataloging-in-Publication Data

Bradford, Scott C.
    Has globalization gone far enough? : the costs of fragmented markets / Scott C. Bradford, Robert Z. Lawrence
        p. cm.
    Includes bibliographical references and index.
    ISBN 0-88132-349-7
    1. International economic integration.
2. Globalization—Economic aspects.
3. Trade blocs. 4. Non-tariff trade barriers.
5. Prices. 6. Markets. 7. Welfare economics.
8. North America—Economic integration.
9. European Union countries—Economic integration. I. Lawrence, Robert Z., 1949–
II. Institute for International Economics (U.S.) III. Title.

HF1418.5.B73 2003
382—dc22
                                    2003062083

The views expressed in this publication are those of the authors. This publication is part of the overall program of the Institute, as endorsed by its Board of Directors, but does not necessarily reflect the views of individual members of the Board or the Advisory Committee.

For our families:

Sharon, Louisa, Alice, Gabriel,
Daniel, and Christina

Nicole, Alexandra, and Natasha

With thanks for love and support.

Contents

Preface

How important are the remaining barriers to international trade? What benefits might be expected if they were removed? The answers to these questions are crucial when considering whether additional efforts at international integration are worthwhile. Major current initiatives, such as multilateral trade liberalization in the Doha Round and the efforts to complete the European Common Market, imply that additional integration is highly desirable, while the widespread use of the term "globalization" to describe our era suggests that it is already almost complete.

Significant difficulties confront researchers who wish to give compelling answers to these questions. When tariffs were high, we could assume that they accounted for the most important costs of protection. It was then a relatively simple matter to use economic models to estimate these costs. But it has become increasingly apparent that, even when tariffs are eliminated, national borders continue to segment markets. This debate over globalization had a precursor in an earlier debate over the Japanese market. In that case too the issue was not tariffs but the role of "invisible barriers," which allegedly prevented imports of foreign goods and services.

Various methods have been used to try to capture the effects of invisible barriers, but comparisons of price differentials are surely the most plausible. This is a difficult task because it is not easy to find prices that are comparable, comprehensive, and not distorted by retail and wholesale distribution margins. In this book, Scott Bradford and Robert Lawrence have done so. This allows them to estimate ex-factory prices across the OECD countries for goods (not services). In a fully integrated market, subject to transportation costs, these are the prices we would expect to converge.

Bradford and Lawrence find, however, that significant barriers still remain. They then use a computable general equilibrium model to simulate the impact of full traded-goods price convergence on national income. Using this original approach, the authors then answer a series of key policy questions: Is Japan becoming more open? Is Europe becoming a single market? How integrated are the United States and Canada?

The authors' central finding is that there is considerable international market fragmentation among industrial countries. Firms charge different prices for similar products in different national markets, even among countries with low tariffs. The authors also find that the efficiency gains from integration would be considerably larger than the gains typically estimated solely from eliminating remaining border barriers.

Bradford and Lawrence estimate that integration among the eight countries in their sample—Australia, Canada, Germany, Italy, Japan, the Netherlands, the United Kingdom, and the United States—would raise global GDP by more than $500 billion. This would increase the size of the world economy by over 2 percent. Remarkably, almost half the global gain in these eight countries could be reaped if Japan alone eliminated its international fragmentation.

This study is the most recent in a large number produced by the Institute that estimate the economic results of further international integration. Earlier efforts include *The Benefits of Price Convergence: Speculative Calculations* (2002) by Gary Clyde Hufbauer, Erika Wada, and Tony Warren and a series directed by Dr. Hufbauer to estimate the impact of trade protection in each of the world's major trading areas: *Measuring the Costs of Protection in Europe* (2001) by Patrick Messerlin; *Measuring the Costs of Protection in China* (1998) by Zhang Shuguang, Zhang Yansheng, and Wan Zhongxin; *Measuring the Costs of Visible Protection in Korea* (1996) by Namdoo Kim; *Measuring the Costs of Protection in Japan* (1995) by Yoko Sazanami, Shujiro Urata, and Hiroki Kawai; and *Measuring the Costs of Protection in the United States* (1994) by Hufbauer and Kimberly Ann Elliott. We hope that all these analyses will continue to contribute positively to the ongoing debate over the merits of further globalization.

The Institute for International Economics is a private nonprofit institution for the study and discussion of international economic policy. Its purpose is to analyze important issues in that area and to develop and communicate practical new approaches for dealing with them. The Institute is completely nonpartisan.

The Institute is funded largely by philanthropic foundations. Major institutional grants are now being received from the William M. Keck, Jr. Foundation and the Starr Foundation. A number of other foundations and private corporations contribute to the highly diversified financial resources of the Institute. About 18 percent of the Institute's resources in our latest fiscal year were provided by contributors outside the United States, including about 8 percent from Japan.

The Board of Directors bears overall responsibilities for the Institute and gives general guidance and approval to its research program, including the identification of topics that are likely to become important over the medium run (one to three years), and which should be addressed by the Institute. The director, working closely with the staff and outside Advisory Committee, is responsible for the development of particular projects and makes the final decision to publish an individual study.

The Institute hopes that its studies and other activities will contribute to building a stronger foundation for international economic policy around the world. We invite readers of these publications to let us know how they think we can best accomplish this objective.

C. FRED BERGSTEN
Director
January 2004

Acknowledgments

We heartily thank many who have made this book possible. We are grateful to C. Fred Bergsten for his encouragement and patience. Zach Grubler and Fernanda Sayavedra provided top-notch research assistance. Francette Koechlin of the OECD supplied the crucial price data upon which this study depends and graciously answered numerous questions. Various input-output data experts helped greatly: Wendy Bibo of the Australian Bureau of Statistics; Luc Avonds of Belgium's Federaal Planbureau; Ronald Rioux of Statistics Canada; Peter Bleses of Germany's Federal Statistical Office; Anna Rita Dionisi of Italy's National Institute of Statistics; Ian Gouldson and Sanjiv Mahajan of the United Kingdom's Office for National Statistics; and Mark Planting and Robert Rabinowitz of the US Department of Commerce, Bureau of Economic Analysis. Seminar participants at an Institute for International Economics seminar in November 2002 gave valuable input. Two anonymous referees gave detailed, thoughtful, and helpful comments. Mike Treadway's editing significantly improved the manuscript. Marla Banov and Madona Devasahayam skillfully guided the book—and us—through the final stages of publication. We gratefully acknowledge funding from the Brigham Young University College of Family, Home, and Social Sciences.

1

Introduction

How important are the remaining barriers to international integration in goods markets? How would eliminating them affect global welfare and the welfare of countries individually? Is Japan becoming more open? Is Europe becoming a single market? How integrated are the United States and Canada? In this study we attempt to answer these questions, using the most comprehensive price data available.

Globalization is the word perhaps most commonly used to describe the present era. Advanced communications and cheaper transportation have dramatically reduced the importance of geography; lower tariffs and the elimination of many import quotas have reduced the importance of trade barriers at the border. To be sure, differences in national laws and regulatory systems still create frictions, but increasingly, international agreements constrain even these differences. Once virtually confined to tariff reductions in goods trade, the scope of trade agreements has been broadened and deepened. Now the multilateral trading rules include trade in services. They also cover government procurement, customs procedures, standards, certification procedures, intellectual property, and binding dispute settlement.

Yet the notion that more integration is needed still drives policy. The Doha Round of multilateral trade negotiations launched by the World Trade Organization aims at improving market access, particularly in agriculture and services. It might also initiate additional negotiations to deepen integration of the multilateral system further, with new rules covering competition policies, investment, the environment, and trade facilitation. In addition, countries continue to negotiate regional agreements, many covering behind-the-border measures as well as traditional barriers to trade at the border.

Among world regions, the European Union has moved the furthest toward eliminating national borders: efforts to complete the internal market by 1992 included mutual recognition of national regulations, some harmonization of standards, and the implementation of common policies by the European Commission. The European Union has also implemented a program for economic and monetary union, highlighted by the launch of a common currency, the euro, in 2002. Nonetheless, many in Europe still believe that further deepening is required, and efforts to promote European integration continue.[1]

The world's other major economies are also pursuing integration. For the United States, the preferential trade agreements with Canada in 1988 and Mexico in 1994 were just the first steps toward deeper ties with other countries in the Western Hemisphere, through the proposed Free Trade Agreement of the Americas and beyond. In late 2002 the United States concluded new preferential trade agreements with Chile and Singapore and announced its intention to negotiate several more. Japan, too, continues to implement measures to increase its international integration: at home, considerable effort is being focused on making markets more contestable through deregulation; with its trading partners abroad, Japan is negotiating preferential trade agreements.

Yet the idea that globalization should go further does create controversy. The steps already taken to deepen international integration have launched a storm of protests. In the view of their opponents, international agreements excessively constrain the legitimate exercise of national sovereignty and threaten the welfare-enhancing effects of national diversity. Deeper integration is not necessarily better, they say. Harmonizing the wrong policies may be worse than allowing policies to differ as each country decides what policies are most appropriate. When countries have different preferences and circumstances, it is by no means self-evident that harmonized (or minimum) international standards in areas such as product safety, the environment, or the workplace enhance international well-being, even if they remove obstacles to trade (Bhagwati and Hudec 1996, Krugman 1997).

It is not surprising, therefore, that negotiating trade agreements that call for deeper integration has become more contentious and politically difficult. The Uruguay Round of multilateral negotiations, which took almost eight years to conclude, were by far the longest on record. The negotiations for a Multilateral Agreement on Investment among the countries of the Organization for Economic Cooperation and Development (OECD) had to be abandoned. The Doha Round was launched only with great difficulty, after failed efforts at Seattle two years earlier.

---

1. See, for example, "European Single Market Has Boosted Wealth but More Powers Needed," *Financial Times*, January 5, 2003, 4.

Given these considerations, the costs and benefits of further international integration need to be weighed carefully. It is important to know whether reducing the remaining obstacles to integration would yield significant economic benefits. If these benefits are small, perhaps the time has come to place a lower priority on achieving deeper economic integration. On the other hand, if the barriers remain substantial and the benefits great, it could be folly to abandon such efforts, and it may be worthwhile to invest considerable political capital in their elimination.

It is also important to appraise whether previous policies have been effective in enhancing integration. For example, Canada's preferential trade agreements with the United States and Mexico represented a remarkable reorientation of that economy toward the rest of North America in an effort to reap the gains from increased economies of scale. Has Canada succeeded in this quest?

A similar question can be raised about Japan's efforts to open its economy. Is the Japanese economy today as open as other industrial economies? Some observers allege that despite reductions in tariffs and quotas, the Japanese market retains numerous "invisible" obstacles to the entry of foreign products and firms.[2] Government policies that have discriminatory effects, as well as such private practices as the long-term relationships between Japanese firms known as *keiretsu*, are often mentioned as barriers (Lawrence 1991, 1993). These obstacles have particularly vexed Americans, because the United States has a substantial trade deficit with Japan, and many Americans believe that the United States is one of the most open economies in the world. Others argue, on the contrary, that Japan is not all that different, particularly from countries in Europe. While acknowledging that the Japanese economy was highly protected in the 1950s and 1960s, they maintain that over time most of these barriers have been removed.[3]

After more than a decade in which the Japanese economy has stagnated, international interest in Japan's structural barriers has waned. The debate over Japanese trade barriers that was once front-page news

2. For a discussion of the early debate on Japanese barriers, see the papers by Lawrence (1993) and Saxonhouse (1993) in the symposium "Is Japan's Trade Regime Different?" in the *Journal of Economic Perspectives*.

3. Bhagwati and others (Bhagwati 1991, 24–43) contend that Japan is basically as open as other OECD countries. They rely on work by Saxonhouse in particular, who has long held this view. Similarly, many Japanese officials over the years have contended both that Japan is already quite open and that it is moving rapidly toward greater openness. But others point to a wide range of indicators on which Japan remains an outlier: for example, the low share of manufactured goods in its imports and its small amount of intraindustry trade.

In a recent appraisal of barriers in the Japanese economy, Bergsten, Ito, and Noland (2001, 144) concluded that there remains considerable scope for deregulation in Japan. They observed that both Japan and the United States maintain a variety of barriers to trade and that "Japanese barriers are more ubiquitous, but have been declining over time" (156).

internationally has today almost vanished from the headlines. But for the Japanese themselves the question has become increasingly relevant. With meager growth in domestic incomes, many see removing barriers to trade as offering an important channel for improving living standards.

The past decade has seen numerous reports in Japan about price declines—a phenomenon the Japanese refer to as "price destruction." These reports often assign a prominent role to pressure from import competition. They are also taken as indicating the success of Japanese efforts to open the economy and as evidence that domestic markets are undergoing considerable structural change and becoming more contestable. But the overall economic climate of Japan complicates this assessment. Since Japan is experiencing deflation, widespread price declines may simply reflect monetary pressures. It is hard to disentangle the role of structural factors from purely monetary phenomena.[4]

Methodological Approach

This study appraises the movement toward increased integration of goods markets among industrial economies and estimates the welfare benefits of removing the barriers that remain. We are particularly interested in evaluating the progress made toward a single European market, the process of integration between the United States and Canada, and Japan's integration into the world economy.

Investigating these issues is not an easy task. Official border barriers to trade are readily detected and measured: tariffs are transparent, and the effects of quotas can be expressed in terms of their tariff equivalents. Barriers behind the border, however, are opaque, difficult to identify and measure. Rather than try to identify them, therefore, our strategy is to detect their impact through comparisons of prices of goods in different countries.

When markets are integrated rather than segmented, buyers can make their purchases from the countries with the lowest prices, subject only to the additional transport costs of shipping them to their home market.[5] Thus, if international markets are integrated, sellers cannot raise domestic prices above the level that would attract similar goods at a lower

---

4. In fact, disentangling these developments has also presented problems in the Japanese macroeconomic debate since they have given rise to claims that measured Japanese deflation is attributable to structural factors, such as innovations in information technology and increased import competition, rather than monetary policy.

5. Our notion of segmentation corresponds to that of Knetter and Goldberg (1996), who argue, "A market is segmented if the location of the buyers and the sellers influences the terms of the transaction in a substantial way (i.e., by more than the marginal cost of physically moving the good from one location to another)" (3–4).

price from abroad. To obtain a measure of barriers to integration, therefore, we compare domestic prices with those that would prevail if the markets of these countries were integrated in the sense that producer prices could differ by no more than the costs of transportation.

This approach is not new. Other studies have used price differentials as evidence of protection and to estimate the benefits of integration (see, in particular, Hufbauer, Wada, and Warren 2002). This study, however, is distinguished by three important methodological features that should improve the results. First, whereas most other studies have relied on selective and sometimes questionable price data and surveys, we use comprehensive and internationally comparable price data obtained from studies of purchasing power parity. We have explicitly chosen our data with an emphasis on comparability and ability to reflect the full range of products relevant for estimating national income.

Second, we extract distribution margins from the price data. A consumer who buys a good pays not only for the product itself but also for the wholesale, retail, and transportation services required to deliver the good. For example, in the United States in 1993, goods producers received only about 60 percent of the final goods price on average; the remainder went to the distribution system. Ultimately, therefore, the final price paid reflects both the cost of a good as it leaves the factory (the ex factory cost) and the cost of bringing it to market. Although both these cost components play a crucial role in determining living standards, the role played by international trade (and integration) in each component is different. Goods are for the most part tradable internationally, and in a fully integrated market, after transport costs are subtracted, producer prices should converge; that is, wholesalers throughout the market should be able to purchase them at the lowest possible price. By contrast, distribution systems are heavily location-specific and thus nontradable. To be sure, consumers can use mail-order and now the Internet when buying goods internationally, bypassing the traditional wholesale and retail distributors. They can also travel to foreign countries in order to make purchases. But such transactions remain, relatively speaking, the exception. Even in a fully integrated market, therefore, distribution costs can differ across countries—because of differences in distance, types of transport, rents, wages, productivity, and competitive conditions—in ways that fail to give rise to easy arbitrage opportunities. Because many studies of international integration have used retail price data that include domestic distribution costs, they may provide a distorted measure of integration in tradable goods. By contrast, in this study we isolate pure producer prices by using input-output data to extract distribution margins and taxes paid by consumers.

Third, we use a general equilibrium global model to estimate the welfare effects of removing trade barriers. By contrast, many studies have applied a partial equilibrium approach and simply aggregated the welfare

Table 1.1   Aggregate integration measures

Country	Producer prices[a]		Consumer prices[b]		Fragmentation[c]	
	1990	1999	1990	1999	1990	1999
Belgium	1.66	1.70	1.41	1.45	1.42	1.42
Germany	1.61	1.48	1.48	1.38	1.39	1.29
Italy	1.57	1.34	1.44	1.24	1.38	1.21
Netherlands	1.62	1.65	1.36	1.38	1.42	1.41
United Kingdom	1.60	1.78	1.38	1.61	1.41	1.50
Australia	1.50	1.33	1.43	1.29	1.31	1.23
Canada	1.62	1.25	1.52	1.15	1.39	1.17
Japan	1.96	1.93	1.91	2.02	1.67	1.61
United States	1.19	1.24	1.16	1.21	1.16	1.15

a. Ratio of expenditure-weighted imputed ex factory goods prices to the lowest price in the nine countries.
b. Ratio of expenditure-weighted final goods prices to the lowest price in the nine countries (conventional purchasing power measure).
c. Expenditure-weighted ratio of producer prices to landed cost of goods from the country with the lowest producer price in the nine countries.

benefits measured for individual sectors. That approach may lead to estimates that violate aggregate constraints or that overlook the interactions among sectors and countries. Our model allows us to take account of both the interaction of developments in individual sectors and interactions with developments in other countries, in order to estimate the impact of eliminating fragmentation of markets among major developed economies.

Principal Results

Price Differences

Our analysis suggests that international market fragmentation among industrial countries remains considerable, even among countries with low tariff barriers. Firms charge very different prices for similar products in different national markets. Producer prices of comparable goods in adjacent countries in Europe and North America typically differ by about 20 percent, and between countries on different continents they often differ by between 30 and 50 percent. Differences of this magnitude far exceed transport costs. Given these differences, it is not surprising that we find that the efficiency gains from full integration of goods markets among the industrial countries would be considerably larger than the gains typically estimated from eliminating the remaining border barriers.

Table 1.1 shows various measures of integration for the nine countries that make up our sample: Australia, Belgium, Canada, Germany, Italy,

Japan, the Netherlands, the United Kingdom, and the United States. These data are weighted averages of detailed industry-level price comparisons covering about 120 industries. The 1990 data has 94 product categories, and the 1999 data has 112. For each country, we calculated the ratio of each product's price to that product's lowest price among the nine countries. The aggregate numbers in table 1.1 come from calculating the weighted geometric mean of the ratios, using the product share of final expenditure as weights. In 1999 we estimate that US producer prices were on average the lowest in the sample: the average amount by which US prices exceeded the nine-country sample minimum average was 24 percent. Canada's prices were the next lowest (25 percent above the sample minimum average) followed by Australia's (33 percent). European prices ranged between 34 and 78 percent, and Japanese prices were 93 percent above the minimum. These data underscore the relative openness and strength of competitive conditions in North America and the much weaker competitive conditions in Japan and, to a lesser degree, in Europe.

Price data at the consumer level for 1999 tell a similar story (table 1.1). In that year Canada had the lowest consumer prices of the nine countries in the sample. Weighted by share of final expenditure, average Canadian prices were 15 percent higher than the lowest prices available. US prices were the next lowest (21 percent higher than the minimum), followed by those of Italy (24 percent), Australia (29 percent), Germany and the Netherlands (both 38 percent), Belgium (45 percent), and the United Kingdom (61 percent). Finally, Japan had by far the highest consumer prices—on average, prices there were 102 percent above the lowest prices available.

Distribution margins do not explain these high Japanese prices. In 1990, for example, Japanese consumer prices were, on average, 91 percent above the lowest prices in the sample, but Japanese (ex factory) producer prices were similarly high, at 96 percent above the lowest producer prices. International transportation costs do account for some of these differences, but large differences between Japanese and other prices remain. As the next to last column of table 1.1 shows, in 1990 Japanese producer prices were still 67 percent higher, on average, than what it would cost Japanese consumers to purchase goods in the country with the lowest prices in the sample and transport them back to Japan.

Nor do these measures suggest that Japan became more open relative to other countries over the 1990s. Although increased competition and openness, as well as technological progress, may well have added to the downward pressure on Japanese prices, these forces were also operating elsewhere. Compared with the lowest prices in the sample, Japanese relative consumer prices were actually lower in 1990 (91 percent above the lowest) than in 1999 (102 percent above). This calls into question claims that Japan's deflation reflects structural rather than monetary factors and suggests that Japan remains unusually closed.

The largest downward movement in relative prices took place in Canada. Between 1990 and 1999, Canadian relative consumer prices declined from 52 percent above the minimum—the second highest in the sample—to 15 percent.[6] To be sure, the depreciation of the Canadian dollar relative to the US dollar over the period probably played a role. At the aggregate level, however, the percentage decline in Canadian prices relative to US prices exceeded that of the Canadian dollar (21 percent) against the US dollar. Moreover, the convergence process in North America is evident in both aggregate prices and the individual price series: in 1990 aggregate consumer goods prices in Canada were 30 percent above those in the United States; in 1999 they were 5 percent below US prices. Disaggregated into roughly 120 product categories, the data confirm this impression: the mean absolute percentage difference between US and Canadian consumer prices fell from 27 percent in 1990 to 18 percent in 1999. These data also suggest that integration with the United States has intensified competitive pressures in Canada.

Some price convergence also occurred within Europe over the 1990s, although it is necessary to examine the disaggregated price data to discern it. At the aggregate level, in fact, consumer goods prices have actually become less similar. The standard deviation for aggregate consumer prices for the five European countries in the sample (Belgium, Germany, Italy, the Netherlands, and the United Kingdom) increased from 4.5 percent to 13.6 percent. However, the dispersion around these aggregates declined. Our sample of about 120 goods categories indicates that the mean absolute difference of consumer price pairs for the European countries fell from 21 percent in 1990 to 17.5 percent in 1999. The standard deviations of European prices for the 120 goods categories weighted by expenditure shares fell by a sixth. Declines in consumer price dispersion are also evident for all bilateral pairs of European countries in the sample. In 1999 the typical difference between consumer prices in two EU countries was similar to that between prices in the United States and Canada. Our conclusion is that Europe has made progress toward market integration but that the process is by no means complete. There remain remarkable differences, even for food prices, for which, in principle, the Common Agricultural Policy should have equalized input costs. In addition, overall European prices remain relatively high, suggesting that price competition is not as strong as in North America.

---

6. Over the same period, consumer prices in Australia fell from 43 percent above the lowest prices in the sample to 29 percent above. In Italy the corresponding decline was from 44 percent to 24 percent, and in Germany the decline was from 48 percent to 38 percent. There was less change in Belgium and the United States: relative consumer prices rose modestly in those two countries. In the United Kingdom relative consumer prices rose much more, from 38 percent above the lowest in the sample in 1990 to 61 percent above in 1999.

Table 1.2 Welfare benefits of eliminating fragmentation

Country or group benefited	Percent of GDP		Billions of 1997 dollars	
	In own country	In all eight countries	In own country	In all eight countries
Australia	1.61	3.95	5.7	13.9
Canada	1.00	3.49	5.2	18.1
Germany	1.28	2.26	23.2	40.9
Italy	1.97	3.46	20.1	35.3
Japan	3.06	3.27	134.7	144.0
Netherlands	3.84	7.71	11.7	23.5
United Kingdom	3.21	4.29	38.8	51.8
United States	0.40	1.02	30.1	76.7
Developing countries		1.60		103.3
Industrial countries		2.26		450.5
World		2.11		556.8

Welfare Effects

Our simulations indicate substantial benefits from integration among these countries, both for the countries themselves and for their trading partners. Recall that when we simulate integration we do not fully eliminate all price differentials, because transport costs prevent complete equalization. Nonetheless, we estimate that integration among the eight countries (we omit Belgium from this part of the analysis for lack of data), accompanied by removal of their remaining tariff barriers, would raise global GDP by $557 billion (in 1997 dollars) or 2.1 percent.[7] Incomes in these countries, which account for 85 percent of industrial-country output, increase by $404 billion (2.4 percent of their GDP), and incomes in developing countries rise by $103 billion (1.6 percent of their GDP). As a share of GDP, income rises least in the United States (1 percent) and Germany (2.3 percent; table 1.2). All other countries gain at least 3.3 percent of GDP, with the Netherlands enjoying a boost of 7.7 percent.

These gains are far larger than are obtained from traditional estimates of the benefits of trade liberalization.[8] In conventional studies of the costs of protection, the benefits to consumers from removing protection are

---

7. In a provocative back-of-the-envelope analysis, Krugman (1990, 105) imagined a world divided into three regions, each of which imported 10 percent of its consumption. He then assumed that each imposed an external tariff of 100 percent and that this had the effect of reducing its imports by half. He estimated that this would reduce income in the world economy by 2.5 percent. Our results suggest that, with respect to barriers to arbitrage, we are already living in such a world.

8. For example, Anderson et al. (2001) reported global gains of $140 billion (in 1995 dollars) from the removal of all remaining trade barriers in the world's high-income countries, of which $43.1 billion accrues to developing countries. (OECD inflation between 1995 and 1997 was 8.5 percent, according to *OECD Economic Outlook*.)

generally far larger than the society-wide benefits, yet our estimates of the society-wide benefits are actually similar to traditional estimates of consumer benefits.

Moreover, these benefits would be widely shared within countries. Remarkably, in all eight countries, real incomes rise for skilled and unskilled labor, owners of capital (except those in Australia, who suffer small losses), and owners of natural resources (except in Japan). Landowners, particularly those in Australia, Canada, the Netherlands, and the United States, also derive substantial gains. Landowners lose, however, in Italy and the United Kingdom, but especially in Japan, where their incomes decline by 47 percent.

All eight countries derive greater benefits from acting together to eliminate trade barriers than from acting alone, as can be seen by comparing the first two columns in table 1.2. The smallest additional percentage increase is felt by Japan, which would gain almost as much by eliminating its barriers unilaterally. Such unilateral action by Japan would bring both the Japanese and their trading partners large benefits: remarkably, almost half the global gains in the eight countries could be reaped if Japan alone would eliminate its international fragmentation. Doing so would raise Japanese incomes by $135 billion, and it would raise incomes in the other industrial countries and the developing countries by $44 billion and $41 billion, respectively (bottom panel of table 4.1 in chapter 4). An open Japan would raise incomes in the developing world by 0.6 percent, with even larger percentage gains to China (0.8 percent) and the rest of Asia (1.0 percent). The United States would actually derive the same benefits from Japan's unilateral opening (0.4 percent of US GDP) as from its own (top panel of table 4.1). These results all underscore the global interest in a more open Japan. Yet despite the considerable gains a more open Japan would confer on the rest of the world, of all the countries in the sample, Japan itself captures the largest share of the gains from its unilateral opening. The benefits to the rest of the world from unilateral Japanese opening amount to only about 60 percent of the benefits that Japan itself would enjoy (bottom panel of table 4.1).

If the United States alone removed its barriers, the welfare of US residents would improve by 0.4 percent of US GDP (first column of table 1.2). This is a relatively small gain because the United States is already relatively open, the share of trade in US GDP is relatively small, and, because the US economy is so large, such unilateral liberalization worsens the US terms of trade by driving up the prices of the goods the United States imports. Each of the other countries would gain more than the United States because of some combination of higher initial barriers, a larger trade share of GDP, and smaller terms-of-trade effects. The largest percentage gains from eliminating fragmentation unilaterally would be reaped by the Netherlands (3.8 percent of GDP), the United Kingdom (3.2 percent), and Japan (3.1 percent).

Some Caveats

We should emphasize before proceeding that, although we estimate the barriers to international arbitrage in this study, we do not establish exactly what those barriers are. Some may reflect policies that deliberately discriminate against foreign goods. Others, however, may arise simply because national policies are different, and still others may not be the result of policy choices at all. Obstacles of this type could reflect private behavior and institutions that are deeply rooted, such as national differences in language and social networks. These differences suggest, in turn, that although new policies could remove some of these barriers, others could persist despite policy changes. Indeed, it might not even be desirable to eliminate all barriers, since the costs of doing so might outweigh the benefits.

Our estimates of the benefits of integration do not attempt to take account of these costs. In particular, differences in national languages, policies, and institutions may well create barriers to price arbitrage, but they may also provide benefits that would be lost if the world economy were to become deeply integrated in the sense we explore in this study. As Dani Rodrik has emphasized, "Preferences for public goods are heterogeneous across countries and therefore there are costs to harmonization—inability to cater to local preferences—that need to be traded off against trade benefits."[9] In general, each country has an optimal level of public goods such as laws, regulations, and institutions, but this level is likely to differ across countries. As Lawrence, Bressand, and Ito (1996, 58) have noted:

> Deeper integration will allow nations to internalize international spillovers, provide international public goods, police opportunistic national actions, and take advantage of international scale economies. But decentralized national decision-making accommodates diversity in national preferences and conditions, facilitates governmental accountability and is an effective mechanism for giving voice to common historical and cultural experiences in developing communal solidarity. In each policy area judgments need to be made about the relative weights of these considerations.

Although suppressing diversity could thus have costs that we have not accounted for, we may also have understated the costs of the barriers by treating them as if they were tariffs. In fact, removing barriers may actually save resources and therefore yield benefits even larger than our estimates. As Anderson and van Wincoop (2002) have emphasized, trade barriers such as tariffs and quotas generate inefficiency through what are termed deadweight losses, but other kinds of barriers may consume resources directly. A tariff on imported cheese, for example, will raise the

---

9. Quoted in the general discussion of Anderson and van Wincoop (2002, 241–42).

cost to consumers and the price received by producers. Some of the impact will thus simply entail a transfer from consumers to producers and the government. On net, however, there will be a cost to society, because the higher prices will induce less consumption and more production than warranted by the true social cost, as measured by the deadweight cost of protection. The removal of such a barrier will generate efficiency gains. But a second type of barrier may itself consume real resources in addition to causing deadweight losses. These barriers may result from differences in national regulations. Suppose, for example, that two countries have quite similar criteria for the certification of drugs but that each country insists that its own officials certify all drugs consumed within its borders. Firms that wish to sell in both markets must expend real resources to determine and meet foreign requirements. Under these circumstances therefore, in addition to the deadweight gains from removing the barriers, there could be gains from freeing the resources consumed by the unnecessary duplication of regulatory processes.

Two other considerations also suggest that our estimates may be conservative. One is that they ignore the potential benefits from opening up other countries beyond our sample of eight. The other is that they may fail to fully account for additional benefits resulting from increased competition, increased product variety, the reduction of rent seeking, and the full dynamic impact of open markets in stimulating innovation.[10]

A final concern, discussed in appendix 1.1, is what happens when markets are not perfectly competitive. Although, in general, price convergence might have ambiguous results, we believe that when international barriers are removed, prices will converge to the lowest levels and this will enhance welfare.

---

10. This ignores adjustment costs.

Appendix 1.1
Does Price Equalization Improve Welfare?

Under competitive conditions the removal of barriers to arbitrage improves welfare. Assume that two internally competitive markets are separated by a barrier to trade. Assume further that prices in the two markets differ initially. If the markets are then integrated, prices will rise in one market and fall in the other. As prices converge, production in the market with rising prices will increase, and consumption will fall as some of the goods it produces are exported to the second market. It is straightforward to show that, in the market in which prices rise, the gains to producers outweigh the losses to consumers. Conversely, in the market in which prices fall, the gains to consumers outweigh the losses to producers. Thus price convergence necessarily improves overall welfare.

In a world with imperfect competition, however, the welfare implications of price convergence are ambiguous.[11] In this second-best world, if barriers to arbitrage exist, a firm with pricing power will be able to engage in price discrimination. In general, the firm's markup over cost will be a function of the elasticity of demand. At one extreme, if the barriers to arbitrage are removed, the firm could decide to charge all consumers the price formerly charged in the high-price market. Consumers and profits in that market would be unaffected, but consumers in the low-price market would lose. In addition, the firm would earn lower profits from those consumers. Thus welfare would decline.[12] At the other extreme, however, the price could fall to the level in the low-price market. Under these circumstances profits and welfare in that market would be unchanged, whereas in the former high-price market, consumers would gain and profits fall. The gain to consumers, however, will be greater than the firm's losses, and the world is better off. In reality, outcomes somewhere between these two extremes are likely. The result therefore depends on the elasticity of demand in the integrated market.

Assume now that there are several firms engaged in oligopolistic competition. If market demand patterns are similar internationally—to put it technically, if tastes are identical and homothetic—*integration will improve welfare because prices will converge on the lower price.* In general, the demand curve facing the individual producers of differentiated products will reflect both consumer preferences and the availability of substitutes. If market demand elasticities are similar, the residual demand elasticity

---

11. For a more complete discussion see Tirole (1989, 139), who notes, "The welfare effects of third-degree price discrimination are ambiguous. One has to weigh the losses of consumers in low elasticity markets against the gains of those in high elasticity markets and of the producer." For a more detailed exploration with respect to trade, see Malueg and Schwartz (1994).

12. Based on such reasoning, Malueg and Schwartz (1994) argue for banning parallel imports.

facing individual producers will reflect residual elasticities of supply of competitors. The more close substitutes are available, the more elastic that demand will be.[13] Under these circumstances, to the degree that removing barriers to integration increases competition, prices will fall to those in the low-price market.[14] Indeed, if the number of firms increases in the low-price market, prices could actually decline in that market as well. In this model, therefore, price convergence (on the lowest price) is welfare enhancing.

Parallel Imports

Policies on so-called parallel imports have the most direct bearing on the issue of international price discrimination. These policies relate to the importation of goods that enjoy protection under domestic trademarks, copyrights, or patents. For example, such rules govern the importation into the United States of Coca-Cola, which has a US trademark, sold legally abroad.

Countries differ in their approach to this issue. The United States tends to limit such activity, whereas Japan and Australia are more permissive, and Europe lies in between. In the United States, parallel imports are governed by complicated rules. US owners of patents and copyrights are protected from parallel imports. However, trademarked products can be blocked only if it can be shown that they are not identical in quality to the original product.[15] Japan permits parallel imports in patented or trademarked goods unless they are explicitly barred by contract or their original sale was subject to foreign price regulation. Australia allows such imports. The European Union bars parallel imports from outside its borders but allows no restraints on goods that are legitimately resold within those borders. (Exceptions are products placed on the market as a result of compulsory licensing orders.)

What accounts for these policy differences? Maskus (2000) assumes that the United States is a high-price market with inelastic demand and that the US limit on imports is designed to protect US producers and to harm US consumers. He states, "Economies with inelastic demand would face higher prices under price discrimination than under uniform pricing, harming consumers. This surely explains the limited permission of

---

13. For a review of these theories, see Waterson (1984, chapter 2).

14. For a study using the residual demand curve as an indicator of competitive pressure, see Knetter and Goldberg (1995).

15. They cannot, however, be blocked if the domestic good and the parallel import are subject to common control, that is, if the goods are sold at home and abroad by firms in a parent-subsidiary relationship, or if both the US and the foreign trademarks are owned by the same entity.

parallel imports into the United States where demands for trademarked goods may be expected to be relatively unresponsive to price" (Maskus 2000, 212). Maskus also argues that countries that are not developers of intellectual property are made worse off by price discrimination and that "this logic underlies the favorable treatment of parallel imports in Australia, Japan and elsewhere." But the evidence in this paper suggests an alternative, more benign view of these policies. The United States, as a low-price (and thus high-demand-elasticity) country, could benefit from market segregation because competitive pressures deliver it low prices. Japan has much higher prices (and thus less elastic demand) and benefits from integration. Thus both countries are actually maximizing the welfare of their consumers.

Within the United States, the so-called first sale doctrine is enforced.[16] This means that distribution rights are exhausted when a product is sold outside a vertical distribution chain. US producers are therefore unable to prevent purchasers from reselling their products at a price of their choosing anywhere in the country.[17] We believe that, as a high-price location, Japan should consider adopting even more liberal policies toward parallel imports, and Europe should move toward international rather than regional exhaustion.

In our view, countries with relatively inelastic demand should be particularly interested in allowing, indeed promoting, parallel imports; countries with very elastic demand, on the other hand, have nothing to fear from allowing parallel imports, because their prices will tend to be low in the first place. This logic suggests that, left on their own, parallel imports should be permitted as a way of maximizing consumer welfare.[18]

---

16. This discussion is drawn directly from Maskus (2000).

17. As Maskus (2000, 210) notes, "This is seen as an important policing mechanism for exclusive territories, which are viewed as permissible under anti-trust laws subject to a rule of reason inquiry."

18. This is essentially the logic of Richardson (2002), who demonstrates that when countries choose individually whether or not to prohibit parallel imports, a global Nash equilibrium involves permitting parallel importing into all relevant foreign markets (that is, global uniform pricing).

2

Measuring Barriers and the Benefits of Integration: Existing Studies

The greatest obstacle to measuring the openness of markets accurately today is the fact that countries can, whether deliberately or inadvertently, protect their industries in many different ways that are difficult to measure. Tariffs were once the major obstacle to trade, and their transparency made measurement relatively easy. With the reduction of tariffs, however, measurement issues have become more important as governments continue to protect markets with more opaque, nontariff barriers. Governments also continue to use a variety of less visible but effective means for insulating domestic markets against foreign competition. These hidden barriers include subsidies, biased government procurement, lax antitrust enforcement, health and safety standards and other regulations, burdensome customs procedures, antidumping duties, and threats of protection. Even when not created with protectionist intent, standards can differ internationally, inhibiting arbitrage and allowing producers to engage in price discrimination. Prohibitions on parallel importing (see appendix 1.1) can also facilitate such discrimination. In addition to these policy obstacles, other factors such as transport costs, lack of information, language gaps, and cultural and legal differences may fragment markets. It is also likely that barriers to competition and barriers to trade interact. In markets in which foreign firms (and would-be arbitrageurs) face high entry costs, firms with pricing power will be able to charge high prices.

Approaches to Measuring Trade Barriers

Given the opacity of many trade barriers today, estimating their cost is not straightforward. The exercise must first measure the barriers. For this, three different approaches are commonly used. The first, traditional approach uses explicit measures, for example, official data on tariff and nontariff measures. The strength of this approach is that the barriers themselves, and not just their effects, are identified. The weakness is that many behind-the-border obstacles to trade are overlooked.

A second approach, called the quantity approach, tries to overcome this lacuna and attempts to infer the height of behind-the-border barriers by estimating their impact on trade. A model is used to predict what trade patterns would be in the absence of the barriers, either on the basis of factors such as country size, distance from other countries, and factor endowments, or by comparison with some other benchmark, such as intracountry trade. One popular version of this approach is the use of so-called gravity equations.[1] Deviations of actual outcomes from the effects attributable to the variables that are modeled are taken as indicating the impact of barriers. One problem with this approach is that the results depend greatly on what variables are included in the model. Another is that the barriers are often not explicitly identified. Also, it is necessary to adopt additional assumptions to translate the quantity shortfalls into tariff-equivalent measures.

The third approach uses price differentials. Like the second, this method has the virtue of capturing the full impact of both border and behind-the-border obstacles to trade. Additional virtues are that it is not dependent on any single model and provides tariff-equivalent measures directly. The major problem in applying this approach is obtaining appropriate price measures. In particular, most existing national price surveys are undertaken with a view to comparing the costs of different goods to the consumer. Accordingly, they will include distribution margins, which reflect nontraded inputs. Other problems are ensuring that the products compared in different countries are similar and that they are sufficiently representative of all traded goods.

The next step is to simulate the impact on welfare of removing the barriers. This requires embedding the measures of barriers in an explicit economic model. Results will obviously be sensitive to both the size of the measured barriers and the model that is used. In all cases, estimates must be made of model parameters. In addition, a structure must be imposed on the economy. One important choice is that between general or partial equilibrium estimation techniques. Partial equilibrium approaches have the virtue of being relatively easy to interpret. The problem with them is that they may violate aggregate constraints and identity relationships and fail to incorporate interactive effects across markets. General equilibrium models can deal with these problems, but only by making the models' predictions more difficult to interpret. Results from these models, which often have many hundreds of equations, appear to come out of a black

---

1. For an excellent review of this methodology, see Frankel (1997). For applications see Frankel and Rose (2002), Rose and Engel (2000), and Feenstra, Markusen, and Rose (1998).

box. A second issue relates to assumptions about competitive structure. When markets are competitive, eliminating trade barriers will achieve only the gains from specialization. When they are not, the additional effects that could result from increased competition can be taken into account. In theory, these could raise or reduce the impact (Richardson 1989). A third issue relates to whether the model is static or dynamic. Static estimates, which capture only the benefits of resource reallocation, produce the smallest results. Larger numbers result from incorporating dynamic gains such as induced investment and productivity growth.

Direct Measures

For the most part, border barriers in goods markets in industrial countries are relatively low. (Although protection in services markets appears to be more substantial, it will not be considered here.) According to World Bank estimates, for example, in 1999 US average weighted tariffs were just 3.1 percent for primary products and 2.4 percent for manufactured goods. Similar measures for the European Union were 3.3 and 3.2 percent, respectively, and for Japan, 4.5 and 2.0 percent, respectively.[2] To be sure, tariffs remain high in some sectors in the industrial economies; typically these are labor-intensive sectors such as clothing, textiles and footwear, and agriculture. There are also instances of restrictive quotas on textiles and clothing and agricultural products. Hufbauer and Elliott (1994), for example, estimated that a group of such products that accounted for about 10 percent of US imports in 1990 had tariffs or tariff-equivalent protection averaging 35 percent. Similarly, Messerlin (2001) found that protection remains high in agricultural and labor-intensive goods in Europe. Nonetheless, if these were the only trade barriers, with some exceptions we would not expect to see large price differentials for similar traded goods. Similarly, although the gains could be large relative to the size of the sectors involved,[3] the sectors in question account for small shares of GDP, and therefore one would not expect that removing only directly measured protection would add greatly to national income.

Quantity Evidence

Because all border barriers have been removed within the EU customs union, and almost all such barriers have been removed between Canada and the United States, focusing only on border barriers would lead to the conclusion that no further gains are to be had from regional integration,

---

2. As reported in Bergsten, Ito, and Noland (2001, 125).

3. For example, in the United States, Hufbauer, Wada, and Warren (2002) estimated that the consumer cost per job saved was $170,000.

and only limited gains from eliminating the remaining barriers to external trade. But the idea that, even in these well-established free trade areas, the only remaining barriers to trade are border barriers and transport costs is hard to square with other evidence.[4]

One line of inquiry that has produced such evidence uses the gravity model, which controls for the impacts of a country's income and distance from its trading partners in explaining its trade volumes. Studies using this approach generally indicate that additional border effects exist and are significant.[5] McCallum (1995) found, for example, that after controlling for distance and size, trade between two Canadian provinces in 1988–90 was on average more than 20 times larger than average trade between a Canadian province and a US state. Others have replicated these findings qualitatively, although the size of the effect is sensitive to the period examined and the precise specification of the model. Using data for 1993–96, Helliwell (1998) found that this unexplained Canadian home bias had fallen to a factor of 12, and Anderson and van Wincoop (2002) found a factor of 6. Wei (1996) extended the analysis to other OECD countries. Using a different specification,[6] he found that the typical OECD country tends to "import" two and a half times as much from itself as from an otherwise identical country. Wei also found that this home bias has declined over time, albeit very slowly.[7] Overall, according to Obstfeld and Rogoff (2000, 4), "a balanced interpretation of the literature is that countries do exhibit a considerable degree of home bias, but the bias is not as extreme as McCallum's original estimates suggested."

Nonetheless, this finding of home bias leaves important questions unanswered. One relates to the role played by differences in consumer preferences. If goods are differentiated and consumers prefer domestic varieties, home bias could exist even in the absence of border effects.[8] A

---

4. For the United States, in 2001, the costs of transportation, insurance, and freight amounted to only 4.2 percent of the value of imports.

5. In its basic form, the gravity model consists of an equation in which, much like the physical equation for gravity, the linkage between two bodies (countries) is explained by their masses (national income) and the distance between them. The equation can be specified in linear form when the variables are expressed as logarithms. Thus we have $T_{ij} = a_1 + a_2 \ln Y_i + a_3 \ln Y_j + a_4 \ln(\text{Dist}_{ij}) + a_5 B + E_{ij}$, where T_{ij} is trade between two countries i and j, Y is income, Dist_{ij} is the distance between them, B stands for any other variable or variables whose impact the researcher seeks to measure, and E_{ij} is a random error term.

6. In his equations, in addition to controlling for distance and size, Wei added controls for language and for whether countries are adjacent, and, to introduce other than bilateral considerations, he included a measure of remoteness, namely, average distance from other trading partners.

7. Evans (1998) obtained results that lie between those of Wei and Helliwell.

8. Head and Mayer (1999) claimed that diversity in national and regional tastes are important in European home bias.

second issue relates to the height of the barriers. As Evans (1998) pointed out, the existence of fairly large home bias in buying patterns does not necessarily indicate large barriers to arbitrage. She noted that if demand is very elastic, barriers that are quite small could give rise to volume effects that are fairly large. Moreover, the welfare effects of such barriers need not be large. However, the less elastic is demand, the larger the barrier required to generate any particular degree of home bias, and the larger the welfare costs associated with given volume shortfalls. Employing this reasoning, Obstfeld and Rogoff (2000) claimed that the home bias puzzle could be solved if there are only small border frictions but sufficiently high (but still plausible) elasticities of substitution. But other studies based on gravity equations reach different conclusions. For example, Evans (2001) found that, with elasticities of substitution between 5 and 8, the impact of the border is equivalent to a tariff of between 51 and 105 percent, depending on the industry. Similarly, Anderson and van Wincoop (2002) estimated, based on an elasticity of substitution of 5, that the border barriers between the United States and Canada are equivalent to a tariff of 49 percent and that, even if the elasticity of substitution were 10, the border barriers would still be equivalent to roughly a 20 percent tariff. Head and Mayer (1999) estimated that, even with an elasticity of 8, within-Europe border effects have a tariff equivalent of 45 percent. Finally, even Obstfeld and Rogoff acknowledged that solving the home bias problem in this way does not allow one to explain the evidence provided by studies of international price behavior that points to much higher border effects.[9]

Price Evidence

If goods are perfect substitutes for each other, they should sell for the same price in an integrated market. This is sometimes referred to as the law of one price. In the short run, prices may well differ until markets adjust, but over the long run, arbitrage should remove any tendency for prices to diverge. This should be the case even where the product is supplied by a monopolist. As Knetter and Goldberg (1995, 4) observed, "A monopoly supplier may charge a price above marginal cost, but be incapable of price discrimination if buyers are well organized or the product is easily transported across markets." The absence of price convergence therefore suggests the presence of barriers. Market segmentation due to distance, tariffs, or other barriers, for example, could cause international prices to differ permanently, but by no more than their impact on the

---

9. "We cannot claim the degree of success in elucidating pricing puzzles as in the case of quantity puzzles, at least not with the kind of very simple models we have featured here" (42). Obstfeld and Rogoff also discussed the need to build in a distinction between retail and wholesale price levels.

costs of arbitrage.[10] Thus differences in the international prices of similar goods provide a measure of the tariff equivalence of barriers.

If barriers are relatively small, therefore, it should not be possible for producers to charge different prices in international markets. If home bias reflects a combination of low barriers and goods that are close substitutes, deviations from the law of one price should be relatively small and short-lived. Yet a large number of studies, using a variety of methodologies and asking somewhat different questions, find that international market segmentation is significant.

One set of studies has explored whether the law of one price holds for specific commodities. These studies have generally found deviations that are large and persistent. The classic study of this question was by Isard (1977), who speculated that nominal exchange rate changes were an important reason for these deviations. Since then his results have been replicated many times, for example, by Richardson (1978) and Giovannini (1988). Froot, Kim, and Rogoff (1995) obtained data on eight commodities in England and Holland over a 700-year period and found that the substantial deviations from the law of one price are no smaller or less persistent today than they were in the past.

A second set of studies explores the pass-through of exchange rate changes. Generally, these studies report that, when exchange rates change, the resulting changes in domestic-currency costs are not fully passed through to the prices charged in foreign currencies. Pass-through for US imports is typically on the order of 50 to 60 percent.[11] A related phenomenon is that firms engage in international price discrimination, charging different prices in different markets for the same product. Knetter (1989) studied unit values, for exports at a highly disaggregated level, from a single source to different destinations, and found large and volatile differentials when similar goods are shipped to different destinations. Marston (1990), using a model of a price-discriminating monopolist selling in a domestic and an export market, found similar evidence in Japanese data. Another interesting study is that undertaken by Haskal and Wolf (2001), who explored pricing by a single multinational furniture retailer and found that price deviations across branches in different countries for the same product were typically between 20 and 50 percent. They also found that differences in local costs (such as distribution costs and taxes) did not account for these deviations, and they ascribed them instead to strategic pricing behavior.

Presumably, firms can maintain these price differences only when there are barriers to arbitrage. Although individual consumers would probably

---

10. For a review of the theory that prices can fluctuate within a range set by the costs of arbitrage, see O'Connell and Wei (2000).

11. According to Knetter and Goldberg (1996), for the United States, pass-through appears to be in the neighborhood of 60 percent. For other countries it appears to be higher.

find it too costly to engage in international comparison shopping for most goods, the fact that wholesalers do not eliminate these differences implies the presence of substantial barriers. In addition to government policies, manufacturers can contribute to such barriers by enforcing marketing contracts, providing location-specific warranties and service, and other mechanisms. Location-specific standards also facilitate their efforts.

A third group of studies explores the relationship between nominal exchange rate changes and purchasing power parity (PPP).[12] Generally, these studies seek to test for an association between nominal exchange rate changes and relative inflation rates; thus they test what is sometimes termed "relative" rather than "absolute" PPP. All prices in the United States could be half those in Japan (and thus absolute PPP would be absent), but if US inflation is 10 percent higher than Japanese inflation, and in the same period the yen appreciates by 10 percent, relative PPP would hold.[13]

There is some evidence that, over the very long run, exchange rates converge to absolute PPP, but the adjustment appears remarkably slow. According to Rogoff (1996, 647), "A number of recent studies have weighed in with fairly persuasive evidence that real exchange rates tend toward purchasing power parity in the long run. Consensus estimates suggest however that the speed of convergence to PPP is extremely slow; deviations appear to damp out at the rate of roughly 15 percent per year." For our purposes these results are interesting because (assuming price indexes all have similar weights) PPP is a necessary if not a sufficient condition for markets to be fully integrated. If PPP fails to hold, it means that, when converted into the same currency, similar goods persistently sell for different prices. This persistence suggests that, if there are no barriers, profitable arbitrage opportunities remain.[14]

A fourth set of studies explores relative price variability. These are tests for what Engel and Rogers (1996) have termed the proportional law of one price. Examining prices in 14 consumption categories for 23 Canadian and US cities, they found that distance significantly affects the monthly variability of relative prices but, in addition, that variability is much higher between cities separated by a border. They concluded that the effect of a border on price variability is equivalent to that of adding between 2,500 and 10,000 miles between cities in the same country. Similarly, Parsley and Wei (1996) examined price data for 51 final goods obtained from local chamber of commerce staff and found that domestic tradable goods prices converge rapidly. They also concluded that distance

---

12. For an excellent review see Rogoff (1996).

13. Technically, these are actually tests of nominal neutrality.

14. The evidence on convergence within countries is more mixed. Parsley and Wei (1996) estimated a half-life of only about one year. Cecchetti, Nelson, and Sonora (2002) found quite long half-lives using long-term consumer price data for US cities.

alone cannot explain why convergence is faster within the United States than across countries. Parsley and Wei (2000), using data on prices for 27 traded goods across 96 cities in the United States and Japan,[15] confirmed the vast difference in speeds of intracountry and international relative price adjustments.[16] The same authors (Parsley and Wei, 2001), using disaggregated data for 95 goods in 83 cities between 1990 and 2000, found that goods market integration increases over time.

Most studies use price observations taken at the retail level. Even for goods, these will include an element of nontradable value added. This leads naturally to the question of whether this nontradable element helps explain departures from PPP. In an effort to sort this question out, several studies have compared the covariability of prices of goods and services. In fact, Engel and Rogers (1997) found that covariability is actually lower for goods than for services, suggesting that perhaps the services or nontraded component in final goods prices drives prices toward rather than away from PPP. However, as they noted, this result could also reflect the greater volatility of goods prices.

The most important source of relative price variability in these studies generally turns out to be the nominal exchange rate.[17] But this is not a full explanation. If the same good sells for different prices when expressed in a common currency, why is there no arbitrage? Although the exchange rate change could well induce the price difference, the persistence of such differences implies that an additional barrier must exist.[18]

Overall, therefore, the literature based on price data supports the idea that border barriers are significant. Obstfeld and Rogoff (2000, 40) concluded:

> The traditional thinking is that even though a broad range of goods is non-traded, there is always a broad range of goods that are traded, and these tie down the exchange rate. But a recurring theme here is that the markets for most "traded" goods are not fully integrated, and segmentation due to various trade costs can be quite pervasive. In fact, the spectrum of goods subject to low trade costs may be very narrow.

---

15. The US-Japan border adds significantly to the cross-country volatility of relative prices. Cross-country mean absolute deviations range between 75 and 140 percent, whereas within each country the deviations are between 10 and 15 percent.

16. They did find that the border effect between Japan and the United States declined over time, but this seems to be mainly a phenomenon of the early 1980s.

17. Engel and Rogers (1999) studied prices across the United States and found that sticky-nominal prices play a more important role than distance in inducing deviations in relative prices.

18. Moreover, using only data from the fixed exchange rate period up to 1973, Lawrence (1979) found that within-country variances in inflation rates across US cities were significantly smaller than between-country variances.

Welfare Effects

How large would be the benefits of eliminating these barriers? Hufbauer and Elliott (1994), using a partial equilibrium approach that assumed perfect competition, concluded that eliminating protection in the highly protected sectors of the US economy would have improved US welfare in 1990 by $10.4 billion, or around 0.2 percent of GDP. Consumers in the United States would have gained an estimated $70 billion, or about 1.3 percent of GDP in that year, from removing all US protection, but most of these benefits would have come at the expense of US producers.[19] In 1999 the US International Trade Commission undertook a general equilibrium study that reached very similar results. The study concluded that, in 1996, US border barriers imposed a deadweight loss on the economy of $11 billion.

A study by Messerlin (2001) of the costs of protection in EU goods-producing sectors yielded results of a similar order of magnitude. Following Hufbauer's methodology, Messerlin found that European protection in 1990 cost consumers between 60 billion and 65 billion.[20] Again, however, the benefits of protection to producers are substantial, so that the net welfare benefits for highly protected sectors amount to just 12 billion. Overall, therefore, these results also suggest that although protection may be significant for the most heavily protected sectors, eliminating the remaining protection in goods markets would have a relatively small impact on aggregate welfare in Europe.

Somewhat larger gains have been estimated at the global level for full liberalization of border barriers in goods, but these would require the simultaneous removal of barriers in both industrial and developing countries. Anderson et al. (2001) estimated the gains from liberalization at $254 billion (in 1995 dollars), of which the high-income countries would gain $140 billion and the low-income countries $115 billion (the numbers do not sum to the total because of rounding). This implies gains of 0.58 percent of GDP for the high-income countries, 2.2 percent of GDP for the low-income countries, and, worldwide, 0.87 percent of world GDP.[21]

Although numerous studies have examined the welfare implications of removing border barriers, very few studies have tried to estimate the

---

19. The Institute for International Economics has produced a similar analysis of 25 highly protected sectors in China (Zhang, Zhang, and Wan 1998). The study found that the static consumer gains of removing protection in these sectors would be 1.1 percent of GDP ($35 billion), with efficiency gains of around $5 billion. The authors estimated that if the entire Chinese economy were liberalized, gains to consumers could reach 2.6 percent of GDP. For a similar study of Korea, see Kim (1996).

20. Using a more inclusive definition of protection that takes account of nontariff barriers and antidumping measures, Messerlin calculated that consumers lost 92 billion in 1990.

21. The combined GDP of the OECD countries at 1995 prices and exchange rates was $23.9 trillion, and the International Monetary Fund estimated global GDP in that year at $29 trillion.

welfare effects of either price convergence or other more inclusive measures of border barriers. An important exception, however, is the work by Hufbauer, Wada, and Warren (2002), who have undertaken a pioneering study based on price surveys conducted by the Economist Intelligence Unit.[22] They explored international price differentials and considered what the welfare implications would be if international goods prices were to converge toward the range typically found within the United States. By aggregating results of a partial equilibrium analysis, Hufbauer and his coauthors concluded that, for industrial countries as a group, the benefits could be around 0.60 percent of global GDP. Although the United States, which already has relatively low prices, derives only modest benefits of 0.07 percent of GDP, the boost to GDP in other industrial countries is larger. These authors projected the following gains by country (reported in ascending order): United Kingdom, 0.14 percent of GDP; Canada, 0.21 percent; the Netherlands, 0.49 percent; Australia, 0.84 percent; Germany, 0.99 percent; and Japan, 1.82 percent.

As already discussed, Anderson and van Wincoop (2002) were able to extract tariff-equivalent measures of border barriers by combining their estimates of border effects with assumptions about demand elasticities. They also explored the implications of assuming that these barriers absorb real resources rather than merely generating economic rents. Under the extreme assumption that barriers represent resource costs only, they concluded that the elimination of border effects could have very large benefits, particularly for small countries. Removing border barriers would raise Canada's welfare by 52 percent, US income would rise by 6 percent, and income in the rest of the OECD would rise by 37 percent. Making the more conventional assumption that barriers are like tariffs, generating rents rather than consuming actual resources, they still came up with large numbers: Canada's gains are 30 percent of its GDP, and the rest of the OECD and the United States would see gains of 14 percent and 3 percent, respectively. These two studies clearly indicate very different orders of magnitude for the effects of border barriers, highlighting the importance of further work on this question, a task to which we now turn.

---

22. Another exception is the study of Japan by Sazanami, Urata, and Kawai (1995), discussed in chapter 3.

3

Fragmentation among OECD Countries

In this chapter we analyze three measures of international prices. The first are the final goods prices as provided in the purchasing power parity (PPP) data. (We refer to these as consumer prices, but they also include capital goods.) The second are measures of ex factory prices, which reflect the re-moval of distribution margins and indirect taxes from the final goods prices. We refer to these as producer prices. The third are measures of fragmentation. These incorporate estimates of arbitrage costs due to transportation and shipping. All three measures are reported as ratios to the lowest in the sample.

Data Issues

In the previous chapter we reported the considerable evidence of global fragmentation that is suggested by the price data. However, this evidence may also be questioned. First, there are concerns that some of the studies of the law of one price may not be using prices of products that are strictly comparable. One reason may lie in the fact that data gathered at the retail level may include distribution margins and transportation costs. As Knetter and Goldberg (1996, 8) have noted, "Goods sold in different locations will have different amounts of transportation, distribution and retail-value-added underlying them." A second concern is that even goods with the same name may vary greatly in quality. This is particularly a problem when surveyors have not tried to ensure comparability, or when unit values rather than price data are used.[1]

---

1. See the discussion of Sazanami, Urata, and Kawai (1995) below.

A second issue relates to the comprehensiveness of coverage. Samples of a few products gathered at selected retail outlets may not represent the full array of goods or the modes of distribution through which goods are sold. In particular, many surveys appear to focus heavily on consumer products sold at supermarkets and generally neglect to include capital and intermediate goods. Many international surveys were undertaken to establish differences in the cost of living experienced by business executives and their families in different cities. These naturally focused on a set of products that are not the most appropriate for gauging overall standards of living.

A third issue relates to the use in many studies of price indexes rather than prices of individual goods. Here one concern is that indexes can be used only for testing changes in prices rather than measuring price levels. Another is that indexes taken from different sources may include different products and use different weights in aggregating them. Still another is that indexes may contain both tradable and nontradable goods.

Our Approach

In the analysis that follows, we try to deal with each of these problems. We use data in whose collection every effort has been made to ensure comprehensive coverage and comparability. In addition, we analyze the data at a fairly disaggregated level, to mitigate weighting problems, and we try to eliminate the effects of distribution margins.[2]

We use data on carefully matched retail prices that the OECD collects on a regular basis in order to calculate PPP estimates. With the cooperation of member governments, OECD researchers collect prices on a sample of over 3,000 final goods. The researchers make every effort to ensure that products of the same quality are compared across countries. For most manufactured goods, the same make and model are compared, or comparisons are made from a list of two or more models when each item on that list is thought to be equivalent. For other manufactured goods and food items, researchers rely on exact descriptions of the items to be priced. For example, one description reads, "Fresh chicken eggs, large (weighing at least 680.4 grams per dozen), white or brown shell. Not the best quality but close to it." When they cannot find appropriate matches based on model identification or on descriptions, researchers from the countries involved travel to other countries in order to examine which items would be most appropriate matches for the items in their country. This has occurred with grain, some vegetables, tobacco, textiles, footwear, stationery, and small housewares. The researchers also call upon the expertise of buyers for large stores, manufacturers, and trade associations in order to determine appropriate matches. On occasion, different goods that were deemed "equivalent in use" have been

---

2. See Bradford (2003a) for further discussion and a detailed analysis of the 1993 data.

compared. For instance, 220-volt light bulbs in Europe have been matched with 120-volt bulbs in the United States. Perhaps harder to accept, Japanese noodles have been considered comparable to US spaghetti.

Prices are collected from many markets and outlets at different times during the year in order to obtain a single annual, national average (World Bank 1993, 10). Also, prices of the average-size purchase for the country in question are compared. For example, if milk is bought most frequently by the gallon in country A, and by the half-gallon in country B, the price of a gallon in country A would be compared with the price of two half-gallons in country B. After the data have been collected, apparent mismatches in quality are dealt with by either refining the specifications or discarding the data (OECD 1995, 5). This method does not completely resolve the problem of comparing items of differing quality, but the scale of resources expended on accurate matching indicates that these are excellent measures of price differences for equivalent products.

The researchers aggregate the most detailed price data into categories called "basic headings." A basic heading is defined as "a group of similar well-defined commodities for which a sample of products can be selected that are both representative of their type and of the purchases made in participating countries" (OECD 1995, 5). Thus a basic heading should be neither too broad nor too narrow: it should not be so broad that it results in very different products being compared; it should not be so narrow that few countries in the sample sell it. For instance, seaweed would be too narrow a heading, and food too broad.

In multilateral comparisons, one usually cannot find products that are both representative of the category and typical of what is bought in every country, because consumers in different countries buy different mixes of products. Instead, for each basic heading, each country nominates one or more "representative products," each of which accounts for a large share of that country's expenditure on goods within that basic heading. For instance, cheddar is a representative product for the basic heading "cheese" in France, the Netherlands, and the United Kingdom, but not in Italy. To be included in the survey, each product must be accepted for pricing by at least one other country. It does not have to be nominated as a representative product by another country; it just has to be sold in large enough quantities in another country to be priceable. For instance, cheddar cheese may be priceable in Italy even though it is not representative. Thus not every product is priced in each country. But as long as countries price their own nominated products and a share of all other products nominated, relative prices for each product and country can be calculated indirectly as well as directly. (For details on how the prices are combined into one average price for each country, see Eurostat-OECD PPP Programme 1996.) There are about 200 basic headings. We obtained unpublished basic heading price data from four years—1990, 1993, 1996, and 1999—and trimmed the sample to include just traded goods. The product categories varied somewhat over time, leading to

Box 3.1　Product categories included in sample

Food

Rice	Other animal and vegetable fats
Flour and other cereals	Fresh fruit
Bread	Dried fruit and nuts
Other bakery products	Frozen and preserved fruit and juices
Pasta products	Fresh vegetables
Other cereal products	Dried vegetables
Fresh, frozen, and chilled beef	Frozen vegetables
Fresh, frozen, and chilled veal	Preserved vegetables, juices, soups
Fresh, frozen, and chilled pork	Potatoes and other tuber vegetables
Fresh, frozen, and chilled lamb,	Potato products
mutton, and goat	Raw and refined sugar
Fresh, frozen, and chilled poultry	Coffee and instant coffee
Delicatessen	Tea and other infusions
Other meat preparations, extracts	Cocoa excluding cocoa preparations
Other fresh, frozen, chilled meat	Jams, jellies, honey, and syrups
Fresh, frozen, or deep-frozen fish	Chocolate and cocoa preparations
Dried, smoked, or salted fish	Confectionery
Fresh, frozen, deep-frozen seafood	Edible ice and ice cream
Preserved or processed fish and	Salt, spices, sauces, condiments
seafood	Mineral water
Fresh, pasteurized, sterilized milk	Other soft drinks n.e.c.
Condensed, powdered milk	Spirits and liqueurs
Other milk products excluding cheese	Wine (not fortified or sparkling)
Processed and unprocessed cheese	Beer
Eggs and egg products	Other wines and alcoholic beverages
Butter	Cigarettes
Margarine	Other tobacco products
Edible oils	

Manufactured household goods

Men's clothing	Ladies' footwear
Ladies' clothing	Children's and infants' footwear
Children's clothing	Furniture and fixtures
Infants' clothing	Carpets and other floor coverings
Materials, yarns, accessories, etc.	Household textiles, other furnishings
Men's footwear	Refrigerators and freezers
Washing machines, driers,	Television sets, video recorders, etc.
dishwashers	Record players, cassette
Cookers, hobs, and ovens	recorders, etc.

(*box continues next page*)

changes in the number of traded goods in our sample, as follows: 1990, 94 categories; 1993, 122; 1996, 123; 1999, 112. (Box 3.1 lists the categories.)

In summary, we believe that these price measures improve upon previous measures because they are trustworthy, comprehensive, and internationally comparable. Researchers have long recognized prices as perhaps the most promising tool for assessing protection, but differences in quality have bedeviled attempts to use prices, except for certain homogeneous goods such

Manufactured household goods *(continued)*

Heaters and air conditioners
Vacuum cleaners, polishers, etc.
Other major household appliances
Glassware and tableware
Cutlery and silverware
Motorless kitchen and domestic
   utensils
Motorless garden appliances
Electric bulbs, wires, plugs, etc.
Cleaning and maintenance products
Other nondurable household goods
Drugs and medical preparations
Other medical supplies
Spectacle lenses and contact lenses
Orthopedic and therapeutic
   appliances
Passenger vehicles
Motorcycles and bicycles
Tires, tubes, parts, accessories
Motor fuels, oils, and greases
Radio sets

Cameras and photographic
   equipment
Other durable recreational goods
Records, tapes, cassettes, etc.
Sports goods and camping
   equipment
Games, toys, and hobbies
Films and photographic supplies
Flowers, plants, and shrubs
Pets and related products
Books
Newspapers and other printed
   matter
Durable toilet articles and repairs
Nondurable toilet articles
Jewelry, watches, and their repair
Travel goods and baggage items
Goods for babies, personal
   accessories
Writing and drawing equipment and
   supplies

Capital goods

Structural metal products
Products of boilermaking
Tools and finished metal goods
Agricultural machinery and tractors
Machine tools for metal working
Equipment for mining, metallurgy
Textile machinery
Machinery for food, chemicals,
   rubber
Machinery for working wood, paper
Other machinery and mechanical
   equipment
Office and data processing machines

Precision instruments
Optical instruments, photographic
   equipment
Electrical equipment including lamps
Telecommunication and electrical
   equipment n.e.c.
Electronic equipment, etc.
Motor vehicles and engines
Boats, steamers, tugs, platforms, rigs
Locomotives, vans, wagons
Aircraft and other aeronautical
   equipment
Other transport equipment

n.e.c. = not elsewhere classified

as agricultural products. These data, because they have resulted from intensive multilateral efforts to correct for quality differences, are more trustworthy as accurate measures of true price gaps. In addition, they are comprehensive, covering all traded final goods. Previous studies have tended to limit their coverage to sectors in which protection was thought to exist, without testing whether other sectors might enjoy well-disguised insulation from foreign competition. Finally, many other estimates have been derived only

Table 3.1   Consumer prices in sample countries relative to lowest prices in sample

Country	1990	1993	1996	1999
Belgium	1.41	1.57	1.72	1.45
Germany	1.48	1.67	1.79	1.38
Italy	1.44	1.71	1.47	1.24
Netherlands	1.36	1.64	1.63	1.38
United Kingdom	1.38	1.54	1.51	1.61
Australia	1.43	1.38	1.41	1.29
Canada	1.52	1.32	1.18	1.15
Japan	1.91	2.15	2.36	2.02
United States	1.16	1.13	1.18	1.21
Unweighted mean	1.45	1.57	1.58	1.41

Note: Data are expenditure-weighted average ratios of national final sales goods prices to the lowest price in the sample.

for a single country at a time, making it difficult to rank countries in terms of openness. Our measures use the same data and apply the same method to each country in the sample, thus allowing such rankings.

Consumer Prices

The prices used for estimating PPP are consumer (or final goods) prices. These are appropriate for comparing international living standards— indeed, that is the purpose for which they were gathered. Table 3.1 reports expenditure-weighted averages of these prices for goods in the nine sample countries in four sample years.[3] The lowest price among the nine countries in each category is assigned a value of 1, and the other prices for that category are reported as a ratio to that price. Thus these ratios do not use any one country as a reference. Instead the benchmark varies from product to product, depending on which country has the lowest price for that product. As reported in table 3.1, a striking feature of these data is the range of prices that consumers across the OECD pay for various products. The mean consumer goods price ratio in the sample was 1.45, or 45 percent above the lowest price in the sample, in 1990, and 1.41 in 1999. On average, measured in a common currency, in 1999 Canadian consumer prices were the lowest in the group (averaging 15 percent above the lowest sample price). The highest were Japanese consumer prices, at more than twice (102 percent above) the lowest sample price. Other countries with relatively low consumer prices were the United States (21 percent above the lowest), Italy (24 percent above), and Australia (29 percent above).[4] Other

3. The expenditure weights come from the OECD, which calculates them for each of the PPP basic heading categories.

4. Australian relative prices declined over the decade, from 43 percent above the lowest in 1990 to 29 percent in 1999.

Table 3.2 Average absolute deviations in consumer prices between sample countries and country groups (percent)

Country	Between country and European countries in sample[a]		Between country and non-European countries in sample[b]		Between country and all other countries in sample	
	1990	1999	1990	1999	1990	1999
Belgium	18	17	29	30	24	23
Germany	19	16	30	29	24	22
Italy	25	19	34	30	29	24
Netherlands	19	17	30	29	25	23
United Kingdom	23	19	34	28	29	24
Australia	24	24	31	32	27	27
Canada	25	25	29	32	27	28
Japan	45	46	47	54	46	49
United States	30	23	37	30	33	26

a. For example, average absolute deviation of German consumer prices from those in Belgium, Italy, the Netherlands, and the United Kingdom.
b. For example, average absolute deviation of German consumer prices from those in Australia, Canada, Japan, and the United States.

European consumer price levels ranged from 38 percent above the lowest price in Germany to 61 percent above in the United Kingdom. At this aggregate level, therefore, the so-called law of one price certainly does not hold across either the OECD or Europe. Nor is there much evidence of convergence across the OECD over time. The coefficient of variation in consumer price ratios across the countries in the sample was actually lower in 1990 (14 percent) than in 1999 (19 percent).

When the disaggregated product categories are examined, again a picture of considerable variation emerges. We have weighted the standard deviation of each consumer price category by its share in overall expenditure. We find that this measure of dispersion was virtually unchanged between 1990 and 1999, at 0.40 and 0.41, respectively. We also estimated the absolute percentage price differences between pairs of countries (table 3.2). For example, in 1999 the absolute difference between the United States and the other countries in the sample for the 120 price measures averaged 26 percent.[5] Countries clearly have very different consumer prices: on average, the absolute bilateral price difference in the sample was 29 percent in 1990 and 27 percent in 1999. These differentials break down into three tiers.

First, prices in countries on the same continent in our sample typically differed by around 20 percent in 1999. Absolute price differentials between European countries averaged 17.5 percent. (Germany had the smallest differences with other European countries in 1999, averaging 15.7 percent, and the United Kingdom the largest, at 19.5 percent.) Absolute differentials between the United States and Canada were similar at 18.4 percent.

5. The measure is $(|P_i - P_j|)/(0.5P_i + 0.5P_j) * 100$, where i and j index countries.

Second, price differences are larger between countries on different continents than between countries on the same continent. In 1999 the absolute difference in consumer prices between the European countries, on the one hand, and the United States, Australia, and Canada, on the other, averaged 23 percent, 24 percent, and 25 percent, respectively. Australian prices differed from those of all other countries by an average of 27 percent.

Third, Japanese prices are very different from those in other countries. On average, Japanese consumer prices had absolute price differentials with other countries in the sample of 46 percent in 1990 and 49 percent in 1999.[6] Japan's unusual price behavior has a large impact on overall measures of price dispersion at the product level. For the sample as a whole, when product categories are ranked according to the coefficient of variation of their consumer prices, a clear pattern emerges. Prices are most dispersed for food products (beef, cocoa, pasta, potatoes, and cereal products have the largest coefficients of variation) and least dispersed for equipment (photographic equipment, cycles and motorcycles, electronic equipment, boats, locomotives, and aircraft have the smallest). However, this pattern is heavily influenced by the impact of Japan. When Japan is dropped from the sample, the patterns are less clear. Outside of Japan, food prices do not appear to be substantially more dispersed than non-food prices.

Producer Prices

Measures of final goods prices include nontraded value added. These prices may therefore provide an inaccurate picture of market fragmentation, since they include elements that cannot be eliminated through arbitrage. The price of a pound of coffee purchased in a supermarket in Tokyo may be higher than that of a pound of coffee purchased in New York, either because trade barriers raise the wholesale price of coffee, or because the costs of distributing coffee in Tokyo are higher, or both. In this study, since we seek to isolate the role of trade barriers, it is necessary to compare producer or ex factory prices rather than consumer prices.[7] We therefore used data on margins (wholesale trade, retail trade, transportation, and taxes) to convert the consumer price measures to what we refer to as

---

6. These differentials are consistent with the findings of Parsley and Wei (2000).

7. The Japanese Ministry of International Trade and Industry–US Department of Commerce retail price survey (US Department of Commerce 1991) has been used by some to claim evidence of protection in Japan. But retail prices do not reflect protection for producers to the extent that domestic trade margins differ by country. Since we find that margins can vary widely, we do not think that simple comparisons of retail prices provide reliable information about protection. Also, the products for comparison were chosen through political negotiations, so that the final list is not random and does not reflect scientific sampling techniques. See Yager (1991) and Noland (1995), however, for interesting analyses of the results.

producer prices.[8] All of the nine countries in our sample keep track of the detailed margins data that we needed, as part of their input-output tables. Although we originally wanted to include more countries, such as France, in our sample, the availability of detailed margins data determined the countries that were included. We matched these margins with the OECD retail price data and derived estimates of producer prices by peeling off the relevant margins. Thus,

$$p_{ij}{}^{p} = \frac{p_{ij}{}^{c}}{1 + m_{ij}},$$

where:

$p_{ij}{}^{p}$ = the producer price of good i in country j,

$p_{ij}{}^{c}$ = the consumer price of good i in country j, as taken from the OECD data,

m_{ij} = the margin for good i in country j, as taken from the national input-output table.

Unfortunately, margins data only become available with a considerable time lag.[9] The producer price estimates for 1996 and 1999 were therefore obtained by assuming that distribution margins were the same percentage of overall value added as they were in the most recent year for which data were available. The estimates for these years should therefore be treated with some caution, and our analysis of these prices will concentrate on 1990 and 1993.

In these years we actually find more dispersion across producer prices as we do across consumer prices.[10] As reported in table 3.3, in 1993 Japan again stands out as having the highest producer prices (in the aggregate, 96 percent above the lowest) and the United States the lowest (just 16 percent above the lowest in the sample). As in the case of consumer prices, Australia (45 percent) and Canada (47 percent) occupied the next rung, with European producer prices ranging between

---

8. Roningen and Yeats (1976) also used retail prices and adjusted for taxes and transport costs, but they did not adjust for wholesale and retail trade margins, which we find significantly outweigh taxes and transportation.

9. For 1993, 1996, and 1999, the margins data come from the following years: Australia, 1995; Belgium, 1990; Canada, 1990; Germany, 1993; Italy, 1992; Japan, 1995; the Netherlands, 1990; the United Kingdom, 1990; and the United States, 1992. For the 1990 producer price estimates, the data for Australia, Germany, and Japan are also from 1990.

10. When prices are compared with the lowest price in the sample, the standard deviation for aggregate consumer prices is higher than for producer prices: in 1993, for example, standard deviations were 0.29 and 0.25 for consumer and producer prices, respectively. Compared with the lowest price in the sample, however, consumer prices tend to be lower than producer prices. In 1993 the average ratios to the lowest price were 1.57 and 1.64, respectively. Thus the coefficient of variation for consumer prices (19 percent) is actually higher than that for producer prices (16 percent).

Table 3.3 Producer prices in sample countries relative to lowest prices in sample

Country	1990	1993	1996	1999
Belgium	1.66	1.82	2.04	1.70
Germany	1.61	1.75	1.98	1.48
Italy	1.57	1.85	1.62	1.34
Netherlands	1.62	1.80	1.90	1.65
United Kingdom	1.60	1.72	1.68	1.78
Australia	1.50	1.45	1.47	1.33
Canada	1.62	1.47	1.32	1.25
Japan	1.96	1.96	2.28	1.93
United States	1.19	1.16	1.24	1.24
Unweighted mean	1.59	1.66	1.73	1.52

Note: Data are expenditure-weighted average ratios of imputed producer prices to the lowest price in the sample.

75 percent above the lowest sample price in Germany and 85 percent in Italy.

At the aggregate level, in 1993 producer price levels in the nine countries in the sample had a coefficient of variation of 16 percent. However, when the data are disaggregated, they reveal a remarkable amount of dispersion. In 1990, weighted by expenditure shares, producer prices had an average coefficient of variation of 35 percent and do not appear to have narrowed much over the decade. As reported in table 3.4, the mean bilateral absolute producer price differentials in 1990 and 1999 were 33 percent and 31 percent, respectively. Again, as with consumer prices, Japanese prices were the most unusual, with mean absolute producer price differentials in bilateral comparisons with other countries in the sample averaging 47 percent in 1990. In 1990 mean absolute producer price differentials in North America were 35 percent (average of Canada and the United States), and bilateral differentials among the five European countries in the sample averaged 25 percent.

If competition is less than perfect, profit-maximizing firms will determine prices as a markup over marginal cost. That markup will in turn be a function of the elasticity of demand. Everything else being equal, the elasticity of demand will be influenced by the number of firms in the market. Thus, under the assumption that marginal costs are similar internationally, relative domestic prices could be taken as a proxy for competitive pressure. The producer price data suggest that these pressures are greatest in North America and lowest in Japan. They indicate considerable variance across Europe, with the greatest pressure evident in Italy and the least in the United Kingdom.

Fragmentation Measures

Producer prices allow us to get a sense of which industries in which countries have the lowest prices. But inferring the extent of insulation from for-

**Table 3.4   Average absolute deviations in producer prices
between sample countries and country groups** (percent)

Country	Between country and European countries in sample[a]		Between country and non-European countries in sample[b]		Between country and all other countries in sample	
	1990	1999	1990	1999	1990	1999
Belgium	23	23	33	35	28	29
Germany	22	21	33	31	28	26
Italy	26	25	36	32	31	28
Netherlands	25	23	34	34	29	29
United Kingdom	27	24	42	34	35	29
Australia	28	33	35	35	31	34
Canada	29	30	34	33	31	31
Japan	44	41	50	50	47	44
United States	38	31	43	34	40	32
Mean for all eight	29	28	38	35	33	31
EU mean	25	23	36	33	30	28

a. For example, average absolute deviation of German producer prices from those in
  Belgium, Italy, the Netherlands, and the United Kingdom.
b. For example, average absolute deviation of German producer prices from those in
  Australia, Canada, Japan, and the United States.

eign competition requires one more step: taking account of transport costs
from one country's market to another. A foreign good must travel from the
foreign factory to the foreign border and then to the domestic border in
order to compete with a domestic good.[11] Thus one cannot infer protection
simply by comparing producer prices. *The domestic producer price must be
compared with the landed price of the foreign good.* We do not, however, have
import ex factory price data that can be matched with the domestic price
data. So we infer the import price by combining data on export margins,
also available from national input-output tables, with international transport costs. (We have export margins for all countries except the United
Kingdom, for which we used export margins for the Netherlands. Export
margins tend not to vary much by country, and so we feel confident that
using the Netherlands margins does not compromise our results.)

We could obtain detailed data on international transport costs only for
Australia and the United States. Both countries report import values for
detailed commodities both on a basis that includes insurance and freight
(cost plus insurance and freight, or c.i.f.) and on one that does not (f.o.b, or
free on board).[12] The ratio of the two is a good measure of all the costs of

---

11. For a discussion of the importance of export margins, see Rousslang and To (1993).

12. As with the domestic and export margins data mentioned above, these international
transport cost data had to be concorded to the sectors used in our analysis. A concordance
is available from the authors upon request.

shipping goods into these countries. For costs between other countries we simply average the costs of the United States with those of Australia. The ratios for both countries, however, are small, so that the gap between the two is also small. The average for all products for the United States is 1.05, and that for Australia is 1.09. Thus, for each detailed sector, we take the average of the two c.i.f./f.o.b. ratios and use this as an estimate of the international transport cost for that product for all countries.

We use these data on export margins and international transport costs to compute landed prices for each product and country, as follows. Scaling up producer prices with export margins gives export prices for individual products in each country. For each product, scaling up the lowest export price by the common international transport cost gives the landed price. Thus the export price is given by:

$$p^e_{ij} = p^p_{ij}(1 + em_{ij}),$$

where:

p^e_{ij} = the export price of good i for country j,
em_{ij} = the export margin of good i for country j.

The landed price is then given by

$$p^\ell_{ij} = p_{iM}(1 + t_i),$$

where:

p^ℓ_{ij} = the landed price of good i into country j,
t_i = the international transport margin for good i,
p_{iM} = $\min(p^e_{i1}, p^e_{i2}, \ldots, p^e_{i9})$, that is, the lowest of the nine export prices.

We then took the ratio of each country's producer price and the common landed price as our measure of fragmentation. If this ratio was less than 1, we assigned it a value of 1:[13]

$$f_{ij} = \max(p^p_{ij}/p^\ell_{ij}, 1).$$

The landed price could well be higher than the domestic price. For instance, this is always true of the country with the lowest export price. Also, if the gap between the highest and the lowest producer price is less than the sum of the export margin and the international margin for a given product, then the producer price in each country would be lower than the landed price. In such cases we conclude that there is no detectable fragmentation. Thus a country can have a producer price that is higher than

---

13. If these data were based on prices for all producers in the world, a ratio less than 1 would indicate negative protection. Since we are looking at only a subset of countries, however, a ratio less than 1 probably reflects competition from outside the nine countries and thus should not be construed as negative protection.

the lowest producer price in the sample and still have an integrated market, because of the unavoidable costs of shipping goods between countries. Under these circumstances we consider the actual price to be the lowest possible and enter it as unity.

The fragmentation measures tell us how restricted each market is relative to forming a single market with the other eight, not relative to a regime of complete free trade between these countries and the rest of the world. For a given good, these measures will differ from true total protection measures if all of the countries in the sample have barriers to imports for that good. For such goods the calculated landed price will be higher than the true world price to the extent that the low-cost producer has barriers against imports. This may be true of clothing, for instance, against which all these countries have barriers. In practice, however, these fragmentation measures are likely not to differ substantially from true protection measures. If just one of the nine has no barriers to imports in a particular good, our measure of fragmentation will in fact approximate a true measure of protection, because in this case the price in the free-trading country will approximate the world price.

These results are reported in table 3.5. As one would expect, the fragmentation measures are lower than those for consumer and producer prices. This partly reflects transport costs. It also reflects cases when the domestic price is above the lowest foreign price but less than the common landed price, so that fragmentation is set at unity. Overall, the mean fragmentation index in the sample was 12 percent and 11 percent less than the mean producer price average in 1990 and 1999, respectively. It was 4 percent and 6 percent less in those two years, respectively, than the mean consumer price differential, suggesting that, for most countries, relative consumer prices provide a fairly good (but upwardly biased) approximation of fragmentation. Japan is also unusual because its fragmentation index is 20 percent lower than the ratio of its consumer prices to the lowest consumer prices in the sample. Nonetheless, as reported in table 3.5, despite this adjustment, Japan again has the highest measures in all four years that we sample, and the measure falls by only 3 percent between 1990 and 1999. On the other hand, the United States consistently has the lowest measures over the period. In the four sample years, the US measure falls in a tight range between 1.16 and 1.14. The second least fragmented economy in 1999 is Canada (1.17), followed by Italy (1.21) and Australia (1.23). Aside from Italy, measures in the European countries are fairly high in 1999: Germany, 1.29; the Netherlands, 1.41; Belgium, 1.42; and the United Kingdom, 1.50.

We take these measures as capturing the magnitude of existing obstacles to fragmentation and will use them in the next chapter to simulate the benefits of integration. Before proceeding with that analysis, however, we consider the implications of our evidence for the three other issues that

Table 3.5   Fragmentation indexes

Country	1990	1993	1996	1999
Belgium	1.42	1.53	1.65	1.42
Germany	1.39	1.48	1.60	1.29
Italy	1.38	1.55	1.36	1.21
Netherlands	1.42	1.55	1.58	1.41
United Kingdom	1.41	1.50	1.41	1.50
Australia	1.31	1.29	1.29	1.23
Canada	1.39	1.29	1.18	1.17
Japan	1.67	1.64	1.82	1.61
United States	1.16	1.14	1.14	1.15
Unweighted mean	1.39	1.44	1.45	1.33

Note: Data are expenditure-weighted average ratios of imputed producer prices to the landed price of goods from the country with the lowest price in the sample.

are the focus of the study, namely, European integration, North American integration, and Japanese openness.

European Integration

European countries typically have high levels of trade. According to Frankel (1997, 84), "most of this trade can be explained by the EC members' size, level of development, proximity, common borders and common languages." Using a gravity equation model, he finds that these factors suffice to explain intra-EC trade between 1970 and 1985, without any additional effects that might be ascribed to EC membership. However, he finds that, starting in 1985, membership has a significant impact on trade, and that this impact grows larger in 1990.[14]

Nonetheless, as of the early 1980s, the amount of trade among European countries was certainly less than would occur in a single national market—a concern that led to the initiative to deepen European integration through the EU 1992 program. In their study of the costs of Non-Europe, the European Commission used consumer price data, compiled by Eurostat for calculating PPPs, to evaluate European integration (Emerson et al. 1988, chapter 7). They found that in 1985 there was an average dispersion of 19.4 percent for prices of consumer goods inclusive of taxes, 15.2 percent for consumer goods prices net of taxes, and 12.4 percent for equipment goods net of taxes (Emerson et al. 1988, 150). They also

---

14. Head and Mayer (1999) found that the home bias coefficient for nine European countries declines from around 21 in the late 1970s to 12.7 in 1993–95, but most of the drop occurs before 1986. Indeed, the coefficient on the dummy variable in 1995 is not significantly different from that in 1986. The authors concluded that, when the effect of language is taken out, the European Union appears substantially more integrated than North America.

examined a group of consumer durable goods and found that, on average, price dispersion for these goods across German cities was half that across the European Community as a whole, suggesting that price convergence still had a way to go.[15]

Several recent studies reach similar findings. A study by Head and Mayer (1999) found that European consumers act as if imports from other members are subject to high nontariff barriers on the order of 40 to 50 percent.[16] Official European publications continue to argue that the integration process within Europe is incomplete. According to the European Central Bank (2002, 39), for example, "The data available suggest that price level dispersion for many tradable goods and services remains higher between euro area countries than within individual countries implying that further improvements in the functioning of the Internal Market are possible." According to the European Commission's Directorate-General for Economic and Financial Affairs (2001, 2), "Price dispersion for individual branded products is higher in the EU than in the US." The commission also reported that, in 1998, a comprehensive data set indicated that overall price dispersion in the United States, at 11.8 percent, is lower than the European Union at 14.6 percent. It concluded that "there is scope for further EU price convergence towards US levels especially for tradable products." The commission bolstered its argument by citing a variety of studies. One of these found no convergence in European automobile prices during the 1990s.[17] Another is based on a price survey by Dresdner Kleinwort Benson Research (DKBR), which sampled prices of 56 identical products across the United States and the European Union and found only 4 with greater variation in the United States. DKBR found that it was common practice in the United States to set a single wholesale price and that this was not the case in Europe. Similarly, a *Financial Times* survey of the cost of living across 155 cities worldwide indicated that the dispersion of price levels across 15 EU capital cities was 9.8 percent (the figure for those in the euro area was 7.5 percent), compared with 5.8 percent for the seven US cities surveyed.

---

15. Emerson et al. (1988) estimated the gains from price convergence. The largest gains occur when prices converge on the lowest level attained in the European Community. The gains obtained by multiplying the price reductions by the share of each product in expenditure amount to 6.5 percent of EC GDP for goods. Including some services leads to an estimate of 8.3 percent of GDP. The authors emphasized that these are very mechanical estimates and that they ignore the impact of increased competition on price-cost margins and on innovation. One could add that this approach is surely flawed, since it fails to take account of the fact that lower prices will reduce producer incomes.

16. Head and Mayer (1999) found that border effects are largest for ingestible products—food, beverages, tobacco products, and drugs—and considerably lower for capital goods.

17. Goldberg and Verboven (2001) found similar results: a lack of pass-through, two-thirds of which is due to the local cost component and one-third to changes in markups. Firms keep local prices stable.

Rogers, Hufbauer, and Wada (2001) suggested there has actually been more progress toward convergence than some of these other studies imply.[18] Using cost-of-living data collected by the Economist Intelligence Unit, they found a strong decline in European price dispersion, particularly in the first half of the 1990s, to the point that recent price dispersion for traded goods, although still above that in the United States, is now close to it.[19] Moreover, dispersion of nontradable goods prices was actually higher in the United States than in Europe, apparently because the United States has more variable housing costs.[20] Overall, the literature appears to suggest that European price dispersion has declined, but not quite to the point where the European market mimics the degree of US integration.

Some debate also remains about how to deepen integration. Head and Mayer (1999) questioned the approach used in the EU 1992 project because they were unable to find that explicit nontariff measures, such as differences in regulation and government procurement, help account for home bias. They concluded that it primarily reflects differences in tastes. Others argue that the launch of the euro will go a long way toward reducing remaining barriers. Anderson and van Wincoop (2002) argued that, with an elasticity of substitution among goods equal to 5, the tariff-equivalent of the national money border barrier is 26 percent. However, Lutz (2002) examined four different data sets and did not find that the European Monetary System has led to smaller price differentials.

On the surface, our results accord with those of Crucini, Telmer, and Zachariadis (2000). They examined Eurostat data between 1975 and 1990 and found that equally weighted and CPI-weighted averages of a large number of European goods prices generated relatively accurate predictions of nominal exchange rates, thereby confirming that PPP generally held between European economies. For 1990 we find that aggregated European price levels for consumer goods were remarkably similar (see table 3.6).[21] At the consumer level our calculated price ratios ranged from 1.36 above the lowest in the Netherlands to 1.48 in Germany (table 3.1), with a mean of 1.41 and a coefficient of variation of 3.2 percent. At the producer level, the range was from 1.57 in Italy to 1.66 in Belgium (table

---

18. See also Rogers (2002), who concluded that the level of traded goods price dispersion in Europe is now quite close to that in the United States.

19. The European Commission Directorate-General for Economic and Financial Affairs (2001) found that, between 1985 and 1999, the standard deviation in price levels across the 15 EU countries fell from 21 to 15 percentage points.

20. Knetter and Slaughter (1999) found that the dispersion of prices of McDonald's Big Mac hamburgers and newsstand copies of the *Economist* magazine declined in Europe in the 1970s and 1980s.

21. This result may not be very surprising, given that our sample includes only five quite similar European countries.

Table 3.6 Measures of price dispersion in European countries in sample

Measure	1990	1993	1996	1999
Standard deviation[a]				
Consumer prices	0.24	0.26	0.27	0.20
Producer prices	0.36	0.39	0.41	0.33
Average mean absolute percentage deviation				
Consumer prices	20.8			17.5
Producer prices	24.7			23.4

a. Average standard deviation for each product category, weighted by expenditure share.

3.3), with a mean of 1.61 and a coefficient of variation of 3.4 percent. Aggregate fragmentation indexes were even more tightly concentrated, ranging from 1.38 for Italy to 1.42 for the Netherlands (table 3.5), with a mean of 1.39 and a coefficient of variation of 1.3 percent. From these data one might have concluded that the law of one price actually held for traded European goods and that the European countries were in quite a good position to fix their exchange rates at their existing parities. But the aggregate data conceal a considerable amount of price dispersion.[22] In 1990 the mean absolute difference between pairs of European countries for consumer prices was 21 percent. (Table 3.2 provides data for the individual countries.) As reported in table 3.7, the European countries with the most similar consumer prices were Belgium and the Netherlands (with a 14.9 percent mean absolute difference), with Germany and the Netherlands a close second (15.1 percent). The least similar prices were to be found between Italy and the Netherlands (27.1 percent), with Italy and the United Kingdom a close second (26.8 percent). Producer price pairs were more dispersed, with the greatest price similarities found (in 1990) between Germany and Italy (19.7 percent) and Belgium and the Netherlands (20.4 percent), and the least between Italy and the United Kingdom (27.3 percent). The average for all country pairs was 25 percent.

Over the decade, European aggregate price levels actually diverged. The standard deviation of price level went up from 0.04 to 0.14 and 0.03 to 0.18 for consumer and producer prices, respectively. This took place in the first half of the 1990s, precisely when underlying price differentials seem to have narrowed. Between 1990 and 1996, the coefficient of variation for aggregate consumer prices increased from 3.2 percent to 8.4 percent, and that for producer prices from 2.2 percent to 10.8 percent. By 1999 our consumer price measures ranged from 1.24 in Italy to 1.61 in the United Kingdom, and our producer price measures from 1.34 in Italy to 1.78 in the United Kingdom. Yet it would have been a mistake to conclude

22. This also accords with the findings of Crucini, Telmer, and Zachariadis (2000, 2001).

Table 3.7 Mean absolute differentials of consumer and producer prices between bilateral country pairs

Country	Australia	Belgium	Canada	Germany	Italy	Japan	Netherlands	United Kingdom	United States
Consumer prices, 1999									
Australia	0.0	25.5	21.6	24.2	24.1	53.0	22.3	26.0	21.2
Belgium	25.5	0.0	26.1	13.2	18.2	42.0	16.3	18.9	24.8
Canada	21.6	26.1	0.0	24.2	22.6	56.7	22.4	29.3	18.4
Germany	24.2	13.2	24.2	0.0	16.5	45.1	14.6	18.4	20.9
Italy	24.1	18.2	22.6	16.5	0.0	50.7	18.0	21.7	20.8
Japan	53.0	42.0	56.7	45.1	50.7	0.0	48.8	42.8	51.0
Netherlands	22.3	16.3	22.4	14.6	18.0	48.8	0.0	18.9	22.5
United Kingdom	26.0	18.9	29.3	18.4	21.7	42.8	18.9	0.0	26.2
United States	21.2	24.8	18.4	20.9	20.8	51.0	22.5	26.2	0.0
Producer prices, 1999									
Australia	0.0	36.0	26.9	31.2	29.5	47.3	32.3	36.1	29.5
Belgium	36.0	0.0	35.4	21.4	27.3	33.9	20.4	24.4	33.4
Canada	26.9	35.4	0.0	27.1	24.9	50.3	30.0	34.0	22.2
Germany	31.2	21.4	27.1	0.0	19.7	39.5	22.7	21.4	26.9
Italy	29.5	27.3	24.9	19.7	0.0	46.6	25.2	26.5	26.1
Japan	47.3	33.9	50.3	39.5	46.6	0.0	41.1	43.0	51.1
Netherlands	32.3	20.4	30.0	22.7	25.2	41.1	0.0	24.9	32.0
United Kingdom	36.1	24.4	34.0	21.4	26.5	43.0	24.9	0.0	34.8
United States	29.5	33.4	22.2	26.9	26.1	51.1	32.0	34.8	0.0

Consumer prices, 1990

	Australia	Belgium	Canada	Germany	Italy	Japan	Netherlands	United Kingdom	United States
Australia	0.0	22.4	19.6	22.9	28.3	45.1	21.8	23.2	28.8
Belgium	22.4	0.0	23.4	15.4	21.7	43.5	14.9	22.0	27.9
Canada	19.6	23.4	0.0	24.1	28.8	41.5	25.2	24.8	27.1
Germany	22.9	15.4	24.1	0.0	22.7	44.6	15.1	21.5	28.3
Italy	28.3	21.7	28.8	22.7	0.0	41.0	27.1	26.8	37.5
Japan	45.1	43.5	41.5	44.6	41.0	0.0	46.9	48.1	55.3
Netherlands	21.8	14.9	25.2	15.1	27.1	46.9	0.0	20.5	26.3
United Kingdom	23.2	22.0	24.8	21.5	26.8	48.1	20.5	0.0	28.8
United States	28.8	27.9	27.1	28.3	37.5	55.3	26.3	28.8	0.0

Producer prices, 1990

	Australia	Belgium	Canada	Germany	Italy	Japan	Netherlands	United Kingdom	United States
Australia	0.0	26.5	25.0	27.1	29.6	46.6	24.9	30.5	34.0
Belgium	26.5	0.0	26.5	19.9	23.8	39.3	20.0	26.9	41.1
Canada	25.0	26.5	0.0	27.8	30.0	42.5	28.6	32.6	34.8
Germany	27.1	19.9	27.8	0.0	23.8	42.2	21.6	24.5	34.8
Italy	29.6	23.8	30.0	23.8	0.0	43.4	28.0	30.0	42.6
Japan	46.6	39.3	42.5	42.2	43.4	0.0	45.6	51.2	61.5
Netherlands	24.9	20.0	28.6	21.6	28.0	45.6	0.0	28.4	36.0
United Kingdom	30.5	26.9	32.6	24.5	30.0	51.2	28.4	0.0	37.1
United States	34.0	41.1	34.8	34.8	42.6	61.5	36.0	37.1	0.0

from the aggregate measures that underlying prices had become more dispersed. In fact, the standard deviation across European prices, weighted by expenditure shares, narrowed from 0.24 in 1990 to 0.20 in 1999 for consumer prices and, over the same period, from 0.36 to 0.33 for producer prices (table 3.6). Similarly, the average bilateral absolute price differential fell from 20.8 percent to 17.5 percent for consumer prices and from 24.7 percent to 23.4 percent for producer prices. These data confirm that European markets continued to become more integrated. As reported in table 3.7, as of 1999, Belgian and German consumer prices differed on average by 13 percent, and those in the Netherlands and Germany by 15 percent. Also in 1999, UK consumer prices differed from those in Italy by 22 percent (versus 27 percent nine years earlier), and Italian and Dutch prices differed by just 18 percent (versus 27 percent nine years earlier). We estimate that in 1999, European consumer price differentials, averaging 17.5 percent, were quite similar to those between the United States and Canada (18 percent), and that the differentials in producer prices (23 percent in Europe and 22 percent in North America) were quite similar as well.

Used with caution, the overall level of prices could be an indicator of competitive pressure. Compared with the lowest prices in the sample, average consumer prices in Europe were at the same level in 1990 and 1999: a ratio of 1.41. For producer prices, however, there was a decline from 1.58 to 1.50, suggesting some increase in competitive pressure. Nonetheless, average European prices remained considerably higher than in the United States in 1999 (where the ratios were 1.21 for consumer prices and 1.24 for producer prices), Canada (1.15 and 1.25), and Australia (1.29 and 1.33).

We conclude that Europe has made progress toward market integration but that the process is by no means complete. There remain remarkable differences, even for food prices, even though in principle the Common Agricultural Policy should have equalized input costs. In addition, overall European price levels remain relatively high, suggesting that price competition is not as strong as in North America. As our simulations below will confirm, substantial benefits could accrue from increased integration.

US-Canada Integration

The US-Canada linkages have become the poster child for large border effects. As already noted, in pioneering work, McCallum (1995) found a sizable home bias in the manner in which Canadian provinces traded with each other as compared with their trade with US states of similar economic size and distance. Similarly, Engel and Rogers (1996) found relative price changes to be much more similar within the United States and Canada than between them. Crossing the border, they concluded, had the same impact in raising relative price dispersion as separating locations by 75,000 miles. Helliwell (1997) found even more pronounced border effects at the industry level.[23] These findings are surprising given the proximity of most of the Canadian population to the US border and the lack of physical barriers between the northern US states and most of the Canadian provinces.

Yet the two countries have deepened their integration by concluding a bilateral preferential trade agreement in 1988 and the North American Free Trade Agreement with Mexico in 1994, and there is evidence that the impact of the border may have declined over time.[24] Using aggregate data and a gravity model, Clausing (1995, reported by Frankel 1997, 92) could not find evidence that, in its first five years, the Canada-US agreement had increased bilateral trade. However, on examining data at a more disaggregated level, she found that tariff reductions did have highly significant effects on trade in sectors that had been subject to high tariffs before 1988. Indeed, she concluded that about half the increase in bilateral trade during the period could be ascribed to the Canada-US agreement. Similarly, Helliwell (1997) used new and revised data to extend Macullum's original work to cover US-Canada trade from 1988 to 1996. Macullum had found that intraprovincial trade was 20 times larger than trade between Canadian provinces and US states, after accounting for the effects of differences in economic size and geographic distance. Using revised data, Helliwell found a decline in border effects from about 19 in 1990 to about 12 in 1993 and beyond (Helliwell 1997, 4). He suggested that the effects of the preferential trade agreement might have run their course by 1996 (Helliwell 1997, 113).[25] Engel and Rogers (1996) did not find an independent effect from the agreement, although this work used a short sample period. However, using later data, Engel and Rogers (2000) found that the effects of both the border and distance fell by about 20 percent from before the preferential trade agreement to after.

We find powerful movement toward increased integration over the decade, consistent with the view that increased integration with the US market has had an important impact on the Canadian economy, both in enhancing competition and in bringing prices into line with those in the United States. The single most striking change in the sample over time is

---

23. For example, Helliwell (1997, 35) found border effects to be almost 100 for dairy products; over 80 in fruit, vegetables, and feed; 65 for grains; and 30 for other agricultural commodities.

24. There is also evidence that the Canada-US free trade agreement had an important impact on Canadian manufacturing. Trefler (2001) finds that the agreement boosted productivity in Canadian firms, suggesting a change in competitive conditions in Canada. He also finds short-run effects on worker displacement. For an exploration of the impact of the free trade agreement on an industry scale, see Head and Ries (1997).

25. On the other hand, Rogers and Smith (2001) found that Mexican relative price changes became more similar to those in the United States between 1980 to 1994 but did not find much evidence of convergence from 1988 to 1994 between the United States and Canada.

the decline in relative Canadian prices over the decade. In 1990, in the aggregate, Canadian consumer prices were the second highest of the nine countries in our sample, averaging 52 percent above the lowest in the sample (table 3.1). By 1999, however, Canadian prices were the lowest in the sample: just 15 percent above the lowest on average. Most of the change took place in the first half of the decade, when the Canada-US preferential trade agreement would have been expected to have its greatest effects, but the decline continued from 1996, when Canadian prices were still 18 percent above the lowest in the sample, to 1999.[26]

Canadian producer prices followed a similar pattern of decline (table 3.3). In 1990 Canadian aggregate producer prices, at 62 percent above the lowest in the sample, were far in excess of US levels and, although considerably lower than prices in Japan, were just below those of Belgium and comparable to those in other European countries. By 1999 Canadian prices, at 25 percent above the sample's lowest, were just 1 percentage point higher than prices in the United States. Canada's fragmentation measure also fell from 1.39 in 1990 to 1.17 in 1999, suggesting that, in 1999, Canada was about as integrated globally as the United States (table 3.5).

These relative Canadian price declines at the aggregate level have also been associated with a narrowing of Canada-US price differentials at a disaggregated level. In 1990 the mean absolute percentage differences between Canadian and US consumer and producer prices were 27 percent and 35 percent, respectively—remarkably large differences for countries that had concluded a preferential trade agreement (table 3.8). Indeed, the mean absolute bilateral price differentials between Canada and the United States were about the same as the mean absolute bilateral price differentials for all the countries in the sample: 29 percent and 33 percent for consumer and producer prices, respectively. By 1999, however, the differentials between Canada and the United States had declined to 18 percent and 22 percent for consumer and producer prices, respectively. Those differences are considerably smaller than the average 1999 bilateral differentials for all the countries in our sample, which were 27 percent and 31 percent for consumer and producer prices, respectively. These disaggregated data show that the North American economy has become considerably more integrated. They also highlight that, although there was

---

26. In explaining monthly relative price changes, the literature has placed considerable emphasis on the role of nominal exchange rate changes. In the short run, it is certainly plausible that domestic nominal prices are sticky. However, this effect is less likely to be important over longer periods, when prices are free to adjust. The exchange rate could, perhaps, account for some of the aggregate convergence, but not all. Between 1990 and 1999, the Canadian dollar depreciated by 21 percent against the US dollar. Measured in US dollars, Canadian consumer prices declined by 27 percent relative to US consumer prices over the same period.

Table 3.8   Measures of price convergence between Canada and the United States

Measure and country	1990	1993	1996	1999
Consumer prices[a]				
Canada	1.52	1.32	1.18	1.15
United States	1.16	1.13	1.18	1.21
Difference (percent)	30.1	16.8	−0.4	−4.9
Producer prices[b]				
Canada	1.62	1.47	1.32	1.25
United States	1.19	1.16	1.24	1.24
Difference (percent)	36.2	26.5	5.8	1.3
Fragmentation index[c]				
Canada	1.39	1.29	1.18	1.17
United States	1.16	1.14	1.14	1.15
Difference (percent)	20.1	12.7	3.3	1.5
Disaggregated mean absolute price differential (percent)				
Consumer prices	27.1			18.4
Producer prices	34.8			22.2

a. From table 3.1.
b. From table 3.3.
c. From table 3.5.

PPP in traded goods between Canada and the United States in 1999, sectoral price disparities continued to be fairly pronounced.

Japanese Openness

Official trade barriers in Japan are not significantly higher than those in other industrial countries. In 1999, for example, the average Japanese import-weighted tariff was 2.5 percent—the same as in the United States— and the average tariff on primary products was 4.5 percent, versus 3.1 percent in the United States (Bergsten, Ito, and Noland 2001). The debate about Japan, however, relates to barriers that are more opaque. A number of features of Japan's trade and investment patterns are unusual for a developed economy, including an unusually low share of manufactured goods imports, a low share of intraindustry trade, and low levels of international investment,[27] but there is considerable disagreement over the reasons for these patterns. On one side are those who emphasize the role of natural endowments and other economic factors, such as Japan's relative scarcity of natural resources, remoteness from its trading partners, and relatively high saving rate; on the other are those who see a large role played by both official and nonofficial behavior, which has resulted in discrimination against foreign products and firms. A number of studies have used a variety of

27. For a more complete list see Lawrence (1993).

quantity and price approaches in an effort to resolve the debate. Two early studies, by Saxonhouse (1983) and Leamer (1984), found that Japanese trade patterns were not significantly different from those predicted by a model that explained net exports by relative factor endowments.[28] Saxonhouse argued that these findings suggest that Japanese barriers are not significantly different from those in other industrial countries. However, they could also indicate that the models used are unable to predict trade patterns very accurately. Indeed, Saxonhouse's tests failed to indicate that Japanese trade patterns were distinctive in 1964—a period in which it is widely agreed that the market was actually highly protected (Saxonhouse 1989). There was also evidence on the other side: Lawrence (1987), for example, used a gravity model to explain manufactured goods imports by OECD countries and concluded that Japanese imports of these goods were unusually low,[29] and Noland (1997) controlled for relative factor endowments and cross-national differences in factor productivity and found evidence of unusually low imports.

Price gap studies have also been used to study Japan. Several official surveys have found that traded goods prices are higher in Japan than elsewhere. (For a review see Bergsten and Noland, 1993, 183.) In the context of the Structural Impediments Initiative, for example, a joint survey conducted by the Japanese Ministry of International Trade and Industry (MITI) and the US Department of Commerce in 1991 found that two-thirds of the products covered were on average 37 percent more expensive in Japan than in the United States.[30] However, Saxonhouse (1993) pointed out that these findings applied mainly to foreign products sold in Japan. He claimed that, "in general the prices of Japanese products are not substantially higher in Japan than are the prices of identical products in American and European markets," and he maintained that (overall) "the size of price differentials between Japan and other countries are not distinctively different from the common experience of other major industrialized economies" (Saxonhouse 1993, 29). Saxonhouse (1993, 30) concluded that "the price evidence reviewed here indicates that Japan's market barriers do not differ in degree from those faced when seeking access to other industrialized economies."

This interpretation of the evidence raises some questions about how the quantity and price evidence might be reconciled. If foreign products are subject to higher markups in Japan, why is it that Saxonhouse finds

---

28. In addition, see Saxonhouse (1989, 1993).

29. Lawrence (1987) obtained this result with a model specified in logarithms. Goto (1990) found that Japan is not an outlier when distance is specified linearly.

30. Bergsten and Noland (1993, 182). Noland (1995) found that tariff and nontariff barriers as well as the presence of *keiretsu* contributed to the differences in relative prices between Japan and the United States.

that Japanese trade patterns are normal? This interpretation also conflicts with the views expressed by Ito, for example, who has argued, "The keiretsu or other structures that make vertical restraints and resale price maintenance possible may segregate the Japanese market from the rest of the world. Such segregation makes pricing-to-market behavior possible . . . ." (Ito 1992, 403). It is also contradicted by the evidence found by Sazanami, Urata, and Kawai (1995). They used comparable unit value measures for Japanese imports and domestic factory shipments to estimate the price equivalent of Japanese border barriers. They isolated all those categories in which domestic unit values exceeded import unit values by more than 5 percent—a sample that accounts for 19 percent of imports by value. Overall, for this group, they estimated that protection of these sectors has a tariff equivalence of 178 percent. Using these differentials as measures of protection, they undertook a partial equilibrium analysis and estimated that, in 1989, these barriers cost Japanese consumers between $75 billion and $100 billion, or between 2.6 and 3.8 percent of GNP. They concluded that the deadweight gains from eliminating these barriers would be between $8 billion and $17 billion—about 0.3 to 0.6 percent of GDP.

By using data on producer unit values, Sazanami, Urata, and Kawai obtained a domestic price measure that was free of the impact of the distribution system, and thus a more appropriate benchmark against which import prices can be compared. They were also able to compare a much wider range of products than are included in the usual price surveys and to do so in a way that was not subject to political influence. However, as the authors acknowledged, "unit value comparisons are plagued with statistical difficulties" (Sazanami, Urata, and Kawai 1995, 4). These measures are derived by simply dividing the value of imports (or domestic shipments) by a physical unit of measurement (such as kilograms or yards) or by the number of units imported or shipped. For the estimates to be valid, it is crucial that similar products be compared. If, for example, for a given product type, Japan typically imports goods of lower quality than those produced domestically, this would create serious problems with the measure, since a higher price of domestic goods would reflect higher quality rather than hidden barriers to trade.[31] On the other hand, if foreign exporters apply higher markups on their exports to Japan because of the barriers they face, by removing these barriers Japan might benefit not only from eliminating the distortions they cause, but also from lower import prices. Such pricing is likely if foreign firms have pricing power and if

---

31. Sazanami, Urata, and Kawai (1995) found, for example, that the unit values of radios and televisions produced in Japan were six times higher than the unit values of radios and televisions imported into Japan. The actual level of protection, however, is probably much less than this because Japanese radios and televisions are generally of much higher quality than those that the Japanese import.

Japanese barriers operate like quotas that reduce the demand elasticity faced by importers.[32]

Several of these studies are a decade or more old, and the data they use are even more out of date. There are reasons to believe that conclusions that might have been valid then might no longer hold. Although Parsley and Wei (2000) found evidence of large differences in relative price behavior in the United States and Japan, they also found that these differences have declined over time. In addition, Bergsten, Ito, and Noland (2001) suggested that the estimates obtained by Sazanami, Urata, and Kawai (1995) could now be regarded as setting an upper bound on the costs of Japanese protection, since some of the barriers captured in the price data in 1989 have been reduced or eliminated in the intervening years. Bergsten, Ito, and Noland referred, for example, to a 1999 MITI survey, which found that although the average price for industrial goods (including manufactured goods and services used in manufacturing) was 67 percent higher in Japan than in the United States, more detailed data however suggested that "the prices for manufactured goods were roughly the same in Japan as elsewhere and the differences come from energy and services prices."[33] This is not, however, the implication of a recent study by Hufbauer, Wada, and Warren (2002), who used price data from 1999 and found that price convergence could increase Japanese welfare by 1.8 percent of GDP, a considerably larger effect than the 0.3 to 0.6 percent of GDP suggested by Sazanami, Urata, and Kawai. Thus, even among researchers within the Institute for International Economics, the degree to which Japan is open today appears to be a matter of dispute.

The results of this study suggest that Japan was and remains a considerable outlier. In the aggregate, as reported in table 3.1, Japanese consumer prices were 91.2 percent above the lowest in the sample in 1990, and 102 percent above the lowest in 1999. (The countries with the next highest consumer prices were Canada in 1990 and the United Kingdom in 1999, with prices 52 percent and 61 percent above the lowest in the sample, respectively.)

Japanese distribution margins are sometimes cited as the explanation for these price differences. However, our estimates of Japanese producer prices indicate that, by and large, distribution margins do not contribute much to explaining why relative Japanese prices are so high. In 1990, relative Japanese consumer prices were actually 2 percent lower than relative producer prices. In the three later sample years, relative consumer prices were higher than relative producer prices, but only by an average of about 5 percent. Indeed, this accords with findings by Ito (1992) that

---

32. In a related argument, Hummels and Skiba (2002) showed how higher transportation costs and quota protection can bias trade toward high-quality products.

33. See Hummels and Skiba (2002, 151).

the Japanese and US distribution systems account for similar shares of final value added.[34]

To a greater degree, however, the unusual behavior of Japanese prices does reflect the impact of transport costs. The relative fragmentation measures are substantially lower than both the producer and consumer price estimates. Although Japan continues to have the highest measures of fragmentation in the sample, those measures are on average 20 percent below those for its relative consumer prices.

Between 1990 and 1993, the yen appreciated from 145 to the dollar to 111 to the dollar—a shift of 31 percent. Thereafter it remained in a fairly narrow range, averaging 109 and 114 to the dollar in 1996 and 1999, respectively. Obviously, Japan's traded goods sectors were subject to considerable competitive pressure as a result of the appreciation. Since Japanese producer prices were already 96 percent above the lowest producer prices in the sample, the movement of the exchange rate was clearly in the opposite direction from that required to establish PPP for traded goods. Indeed, in 1990 a yen-dollar exchange rate of 239 would have been required to bring Japanese producer prices in line with those in the United States. Between 1990 and 1993, measured in US dollars, Japanese producer goods prices relative to those in the United States increased by just 3 percent (and Japanese producer goods prices remained roughly 96 percent above the lowest in the sample). During this period, therefore, the exchange rate change was fully reflected in traded goods prices. However, as might be expected, at the consumer price level the story was different. Japanese consumer goods prices rose by 16 percent relative to US consumer prices, and Japanese consumer goods prices increased from 91 percent above the lowest in the sample to 115 percent above. This experience points to the role played by distribution margins, whose costs are likely to be sluggish in domestic currency, and to the importance of extracting distribution margins in appraising barriers to trade.[35]

Between 1993 and 1996 the change in the yen's exchange rate was modest—from 111 to 109 yen to the dollar. Over the same period, however, Japanese relative consumer goods prices rose from 115 percent to

---

34. For a detailed discussion of the Japanese distribution system, see Ito (1992, chapter 13). The fact that Japan's share of distribution in final value added is similar to the United States's does not imply that Japan's distribution system is efficient. Bradford (2002, 2003b) found potentially large welfare gains from increased efficiency in Japan's distribution.

35. We strip out distribution margins to clarify this study's analysis, but this does not mean that we consider distribution to be perfectly nontraded and immune to international competitive pressure. The recent movement of major retailers, such as Wal-Mart, into many different countries clearly shows that distribution is potentially a traded service, and the negotiations under the General Agreement on Trade in Services include distribution services in their coverage.

136 percent above the lowest in the sample and an additional 5 percent relative to US prices. Japanese relative producer prices increased from 96 percent above the lowest in the sample to 128 percent above and increased by 8 percent relative to US prices. Over this period neither the exchange rate nor increased import price competition played a role in Japanese "price destruction." Between 1996 and 1999, on the other hand, Japanese consumer prices declined relative to US consumer prices by 15 percent, and relative to the lowest consumer prices in the sample by 14 percent. Changes in this period are thus compatible with the idea of price destruction, although it remains the case that, compared with the lowest prices in the sample, relative Japanese consumer prices at the end of the decade were somewhat higher than at the start. Under the assumption that distribution margins were the same proportion of total costs in 1999 as in 1996, we can also say that, relative to the lowest prices in the sample, Japanese producer prices were about the same in 1999 as they were in 1990. Over the entire decade, therefore, we observe relative PPP. The domestic currency prices of Japanese producers rose sufficiently slowly to fully offset the 21.4 percent nominal appreciation of the yen from 145 to the dollar in 1990 to 114 in 1999. Japanese producer prices, however, were as far away from absolute PPP in 1999 as they were in 1990.

Exploring price differentials at more disaggregated levels reinforces these conclusions. The bilateral differences between Japanese consumer goods prices and those of other OECD countries in the sample ranged between 41 and 55 percent in 1990 and between 42 and 57 percent in 1999. These differences are markedly higher than those for any other bilateral pair in the sample. With one exception (US and Belgian producer prices in 1990), in both 1990 and 1999, all countries recorded their greatest bilateral price disparities for both producer and consumer prices with Japan. As these numbers indicate, over the decade as a whole, these differentials have not narrowed.

Disaggregation suggests that food prices are one important reason why Japanese prices overall are so high. In 1999, for example, an unweighted measure of Japanese food prices at the consumer level shows that average Japanese food prices were 235 percent above those in other countries, whereas the corresponding figure for nonfood prices was 82 percent. High relative food prices in Japan are also evident in producer prices in 1990 and 1993. Although relative Japanese prices for nonfood items also remained the highest in the sample, food clearly played an important role in the high overall level of Japanese prices. In fact, once we take account of transport costs, we find that, for nonfood products, Japanese fragmentation ratios are similar to those in the United Kingdom. Japanese nonfood fragmentation remains the highest in the sample, but Japan is no longer a conspicuous outlier.

Nonetheless, these fragmentation estimates indicate significant further potential for welfare gains. In the analysis in chapter 4, we argue that

Japanese deadweight benefits from integrating goods markets would equal 2.4 percent of GDP. This estimate is somewhat larger than that of Hufbauer (1.82 percent of GDP) and an order of magnitude larger than the estimates obtained by Sazanami, Urata, and Kawai (1995).

Concluding Comments

We believe that the openness measures we report here are more complete and more accurate than previous ones. Their completeness stems from the use of price gap measures, which make it possible to capture the combined effects of all barriers, explicit and implicit, including any number of regulations and bureaucratic procedures. Previous studies have tended to limit their coverage to sectors in which protection was thought to exist, without testing whether other sectors might also enjoy insulation from foreign competition that was better disguised. Our approach does not allow such preconceptions to limit the analysis. For example, a UN study (United Nations Conference on Trade and Development 1992) analyzed how excess paperwork and cumbersome customs procedures impede the international flow of goods. The study pointed out that these regulations impose not only direct but also indirect costs, such as losses due to deterioration or pilferage while cargo is waiting to be cleared, and the strong disincentive that complicated procedures pose for potential exporters. The study conservatively estimated that these barriers imposed costs of 10 to 15 percent on top of any other trade barriers. Measures of protection that rely on lists of individual barriers, such as the United Nations' own measures of nontariff barriers, will tend to overlook barriers such as these because they are both subtle and ubiquitous: they do not stand out for purposes of list-making. Our method will capture the full protective impact of such bureaucratic frictions, if the low-cost producer in the sample is free of them. To be sure, if the low-cost producer in the sample has such barriers, then our method will only capture the amount by which these barriers in other countries exceed those in the low-cost country. This is better, however, than ignoring them completely. In addition to providing more complete estimates of the effects of various policies, these measures are comprehensive, covering all final goods.

Accuracy in this area of research stems from comparing actual prices of identical or equivalent goods. Until now, researchers have recognized prices as perhaps the most promising tool for assessing protection, but differences in quality have bedeviled attempts to use prices, except for certain homogeneous goods such as agricultural products. The data we use, however, were generated through intensive multilateral efforts to correct for quality differences.

A further advantage of this approach is that it allows us to rank the openness of several countries at once. Many other estimates have been derived for a single country at a time, making such rankings difficult. Our measures, however, use the same data and apply the same method to each country in the sample, leading to rankings in which we can have some confidence.

Finally, in deriving these estimates, we note that there is no necessary connection between tariff equivalents and the amount by which imports are reduced. Quantity changes depend on the elasticities of supply and of demand. Thus a high barrier on a good with a low elasticity of demand may reduce imports by less than a low barrier on a good whose demand is highly elastic. We do not purport, however, to analyze prices and quantities at the same time. These tariff equivalents are simply price gaps. To assess the impact of barriers on quantities traded, and thus on welfare, one needs a model of supply and demand relationships in the sector in question. We claim that the cleanest, most effective way to measure protection is to first derive tariff equivalents, leaving quantity and welfare analysis for the next step. We believe, therefore, that to reject tariff equivalents, as, for example, did Holzman (1969), because they do not tell how much trade flows are reduced, is to tie one's hands unnecessarily. Deardorff and Stern (1998) also concerned themselves with prices and quantities at the same time and became involved in a very detailed taxonomy of various barriers. Tariff equivalents, on the other hand, cleanly capture the combined effects of all kinds of barriers. These price gaps can then be used as inputs in a rigorous welfare analysis, as we do in the general equilibrium modeling in the next chapter.

4

The Welfare Effects of Integration

Having prepared the estimates of fragmentation, we now proceed to consider their welfare implications. For eight of the nine countries, we seek to compare real incomes in the world as it is with one in which barriers are eliminated. (Unfortunately, data problems prevent us from analyzing Belgium separately.) To quantify these effects, we use a global general equilibrium model based on one developed by Glenn Harrison, Thomas F. Rutherford, and David Tarr.[1] The model has considerable country and sectoral detail, with 16 regions and 33 sectors (box 4.1).[2] The model also allows for both increasing returns to scale and dynamic adjustment of the capital stock. In this chapter we first report our results and then describe the model and our methodology.

Welfare Analysis

We conducted three types of simulations of the effects of eliminating fragmentation: unilateral removal of barriers in each of the eight countries to all other countries worldwide; multilateral worldwide removal by all eight countries at once; and a preferential trade agreement in which all

---

1. The model is based on the computer code provided by Harrison, Rutherford, and Tarr. Their code is available for public access at the web.badm.sc.edu/glenn/ur_pub.htm and was used in their 1995, 1996, and 1997 articles.

2. The underlying data come from version 5 (1997) of the Global Trade Analysis Project (GTAP) database. See www.gtap.org for a description and documentation.

Box 4.1 Sectors and regions included in general equilibrium model

Sectors

Fruits, nuts, vegetables	**Textiles**
Other crops	**Wearing apparel**
Other agriculture	**Leather goods**
Live animals	**Lumber and wood products**
Other animal products	**Pulp, paper products, publishing**
Fish	**Coal and petroleum products**
Coal, gas, oil	**Chemicals, plastics, and rubber**
Other minerals	**Nonmetallic mineral products**
Bovine cattle, sheep, goat,	*Primary ferrous metals*
and horse products	*Nonferrous metals*
Other meat products	**Fabricated metal products**
Vegetable oils and fats	**Motor vehicles and parts**
Dairy products	**Electronic equipment**
Processed rice	**Machinery and equipment**
Sugar	**Other manufacturing products**
Other food products	Trade and transport services
Beverages and tobacco products	Other services

Regions

Australia	Rest of Latin America
Japan	Germany
Korea	Italy
China	Netherlands
Rest of Asia	United Kingdom
Canada	Rest of Europe
United States	Middle East
Brazil	Rest of world

Notes: **Boldface** indicates sectors for which protection measures were inserted. *Italics* indicate sectors assumed to have increasing returns to scale.

eight countries simultaneously remove barriers against each other but not against the rest of the world. We focus on changes in equivalent variation (which, given the model structure, are the same as changes in real consumption) as a percentage of GDP. Thus our estimates can be compared with those obtained for deadweight losses in other models.

Here we report and discuss the point estimate predictions for overall welfare changes. The appendix presents confidence intervals for these estimates. Table 4.1 shows the principal results. The table reports the permanent, annual effect of trade opening on consumption once the capital stock has changed to its new equilibrium. Put another way, the table reports the welfare costs, borne at home and abroad, of all protection in the eight countries separately and as a group. The top panel reports these gains as percentages of GDP, and the bottom panel in billions of 1997 US dollars.

All in all, the measured effects are large. Removing trade barriers that are as comprehensive as those we have identified indicates significant benefits from ending fragmentation. As the top panel of table 4.1 shows, each of the countries except the United States would get an annual boost of 1 percent or more to GDP from its own unilateral opening (indicated by the cells in the table on the diagonal). Multilateral opening by all eight would bring even larger gains of at least 3 percent of GDP for all countries except Germany and the United States, and global GDP would rise by 2.1 percent.

Two main forces drive the gains for any given country: the amount of its initial protection and the share of trade in its GDP. The relatively low trade barriers in the United States and its low ratio of trade to GDP mute the predicted gains for that country. Nevertheless, the annual GDP increases of 0.4 percent (for unilateral opening) and 1.0 percent (for multilateral opening) are substantially higher than the 0.07 percent figure obtained by Hufbauer, Wada, and Warren (2002) for the benefits of price convergence for the United States, and than the estimate by Hufbauer and Elliott (1994) of about a 0.1 percent increase in GDP from removing US border barriers. Canada has about the same measured level of fragmentation as the United States but would gain two to three times as much as a percentage of GDP from opening, because Canada's trade share is much higher. Similarly, the Netherlands' high trade share amplifies its gains. On the other hand, Japan's barriers are so high that it reaps substantial gains from international integration despite the fact that Japan has the lowest trade share in the sample: trade accounts for only about 10 percent of Japan's economy. The 3.1 percent boost we estimate for Japan's GDP is considerably greater than the estimate of 1.8 percent of GDP obtained by Hufbauer, Wada, and Warren. Moreover, it is well in line with the total consumer gains (as opposed to just the deadweight gains) estimated by Sazanami, Urata, and Kawai (1995). Another factor at work is changes in the terms of trade. Such effects mute the gains for the United States, Japan, and Germany: these countries account for fairly large shares of total world trade, so that, when they open, they drive up their import prices and drive down their export prices.

The results also highlight some interesting international linkages and interactions. Canada gains more (1.7 percent of GDP) from opening by the United States than it does from its own opening (1.0 percent). Likewise, the Netherlands sees its GDP rise by a larger percentage (1.6 percent) when Germany opens unilaterally than does Germany itself (1.3 percent). The Netherlands also receives substantial boosts from openings in Italy (Dutch GDP rises 0.6 percent) and the United Kingdom (1.0 percent).

Our simulation results suggest that the focus on Japan's relatively closed market has not been misplaced. It is striking that both Australia

Table 4.1 Welfare impact of complete removal of barriers by country and region

Country or region affected	Country or countries removing barriers									
	Australia	Canada	Germany	Italy	Japan	Netherlands	United Kingdom	United States	All eight countries	Eight-country PTA
Percent of GDP										
Australia	1.61	0.02	0.11	0.03	1.66	0.01	0.25	0.27	3.95	4.35
Canada	0.04	1.00	0.03	0.10	0.52	0.01	0.07	1.71	3.49	3.66
Germany	0.03	−0.01	1.28	0.25	−0.04	0.29	0.30	0.12	2.26	1.96
Italy	0.05	0.02	0.66	1.97	0.03	0.10	0.37	0.16	3.46	4.61
Japan	0.04	−0.01	−0.01	0.11	3.06	0.01	0.00	0.12	3.27	2.18
Netherlands	0.05	0.01	1.56	0.58	0.14	3.84	1.03	0.33	7.71	9.38
United Kingdom	0.01	0.03	0.27	0.10	0.23	0.21	3.21	0.21	4.29	2.79
United States	−0.01	0.20	0.01	0.00	0.40	0.01	0.06	0.40	1.02	1.35
China	0.04	0.05	0.12	0.04	0.77	0.02	0.32	0.55	1.49	−0.57
Korea	0.04	0.00	0.03	0.01	0.62	0.06	0.03	0.25	0.96	−0.51
Rest of Asia	0.06	0.02	0.03	0.06	1.03	0.03	0.18	0.49	2.03	−0.81
Brazil	−0.03	0.06	0.18	0.06	0.41	0.03	0.10	0.32	1.05	0.00
Rest of Latin America	0.00	0.01	0.06	0.07	0.55	0.02	0.09	0.86	1.94	−0.53
Rest of Europe	0.02	0.03	0.59	0.20	0.13	0.18	0.47	0.15	1.69	−0.88
Middle East	0.01	0.03	0.35	0.13	0.55	0.10	0.37	0.41	1.96	−0.05
Rest of world	−0.01	−0.01	0.36	0.16	0.43	0.06	0.21	0.11	1.34	0.03

Developing countries	0.01	0.01	0.21	0.09	0.63	0.04	0.15	0.43	1.60	-0.36
Industrial countries	0.04	0.10	0.29	0.17	0.90	0.14	0.35	0.29	2.26	1.76
World	0.04	0.09	0.27	0.16	0.84	0.12	0.31	0.33	2.11	1.25

Billions of dollars

Australia	5.68	0.07	0.39	0.11	5.85	0.04	0.88	0.95	13.93	15.34
Canada	0.21	5.19	0.16	0.52	2.70	0.05	0.36	8.87	18.11	18.99
Germany	0.54	-0.18	23.18	4.53	-0.72	5.25	5.43	2.17	40.93	35.50
Italy	0.51	0.20	6.73	20.08	0.31	1.02	3.77	1.63	35.26	46.98
Japan	1.76	-0.44	-0.44	4.84	134.73	0.44	0.00	5.28	143.98	95.99
Netherlands	0.15	0.03	4.76	1.77	0.43	11.73	3.15	1.01	23.54	28.64
United Kingdom	0.12	0.36	3.26	1.21	2.78	2.54	38.78	2.54	51.83	33.71
United States	-0.75	15.04	0.75	0.00	30.08	0.75	4.51	30.08	76.69	101.51
China	0.35	0.44	1.06	0.35	6.82	0.18	2.83	4.87	13.19	-5.05
Korea	0.16	0.00	0.12	0.04	2.43	0.23	0.12	0.98	3.76	-2.00
Rest of Asia	0.78	0.26	0.39	0.78	13.44	0.39	2.35	6.39	26.48	-10.57
Brazil	-0.20	0.40	1.20	0.40	2.72	0.20	0.66	2.13	6.97	0.00
Rest of Latin America	0.00	0.11	0.66	0.77	6.03	0.22	0.99	9.44	21.28	-5.81
Rest of Europe	0.56	0.84	16.50	5.59	3.63	5.03	13.14	4.19	47.25	-24.60
Middle East	0.06	0.17	1.98	0.74	3.11	0.57	2.09	2.32	11.09	-0.28
Rest of world	-0.15	-0.15	5.57	2.48	6.66	0.93	3.25	1.70	20.74	0.46
Developing countries	0.65	0.65	13.56	5.81	40.67	2.58	9.68	27.76	103.30	-23.24
Industrial countries	7.97	19.93	57.81	33.89	179.40	27.91	69.77	57.81	450.49	350.82
World	10.56	23.75	71.25	42.22	221.67	31.67	81.81	87.08	556.82	329.87

PTA = preferential trade agreement

and the United States would gain about as much from Japan's opening (1.7 and 0.4 percent of GDP, respectively) as they would from their own (1.6 and 0.4 percent, respectively). The benefits to Japan's neighbors would also be considerable, with GDP rising in China, Korea, and the rest of Asia by 0.8 percent, 0.6 percent, and 1.0 percent of GDP, respectively. Developing countries as a group would see their incomes rise by 0.6 percent, and the world by 0.8 percent. Measured in 1997 dollars, Japanese incomes would rise by $135 billion, and Japan's trading partners would see their incomes rise by $87 billion, of which $41 billion would accrue to developing countries. The world as a whole derives more than twice the benefits from Japanese as from US opening. Indeed, unilateral Japanese opening would yield benefits of $222 billion, or roughly 40 percent of the global benefits resulting from all eight countries opening together.

Yet despite the considerable gains that a more open Japan would confer on the rest of the world, of all the countries in the sample, Japan itself captures the largest share of the gains from its unilateral opening. The benefits to the rest of the world from unilateral Japanese opening amount to about 60 percent of the benefits enjoyed by Japan itself. Similarly, Japan gains only an additional 7.5 percent (the smallest additional percentage increase) when all eight countries open together than when it opens unilaterally. The unilateral opening of Japan would therefore be a win-win policy. Japan would reap most of the benefits, but the gains to the world would also be sizable.

Developing countries would also reap significant gains from unilateral US opening, equal to 0.4 percent of GDP, or about $28 billion in 1997 dollars. The United States is the only country in the sample whose barriers have a larger percentage impact on developing-country incomes than on those in other industrialized countries. Unlike the rest of Latin America, however, Brazil would benefit more from Japanese opening (GDP would rise by 0.4 percent) than from US opening (0.3 percent). The trade barriers of both Japan and the United States impose costs on lower-income countries that more than cancel out the annual development aid they give.

Although all countries gain more from multilateral opening than from unilateral opening, Australia, Canada, and the United States receive especially large extra payoffs: their gains from multilateral removal of barriers are about 2.5 times or more the unilateral gains. Not surprisingly, these three countries have the lowest barriers. They thus have an especially large incentive to engage in multilateral trade reform as opposed to unilateral opening. Nonetheless, when these countries do open, they confer far larger benefits on the rest of the world than they derive themselves. Indeed, the global benefits that would result from Canada's opening are 4.6 times as large as the benefits realized by Canada itself. For the United States and Australia, the ratios are 2.9 and 1.9, respectively. German unilateral liberalization would confer global benefits that are three times as large as Germany itself captures.

Five of the eight countries in the sample actually do better with a preferential trade agreement (PTA) among the group than with multilateral removal of all barriers against the rest of the world. The exceptions are Germany, Japan, and the United Kingdom. Apparently these three countries gain proportionately more from trade with countries outside the sample than do the other five. Developing countries, however, lose from such an exclusionary arrangement. Instead of the 1.6 percent of GDP gain they would experience from multilateral opening by all eight sample countries, developing countries would lose 0.4 percent from such a PTA.

Anderson et al. (2001) present a simulation in which all countries remove all (traditional) global trade barriers that remain after the Uruguay Round. They conclude that the benefits of such removal would have amounted to $254 billion in 1995. They also estimate that the global benefits from removing barriers in the high-income countries alone would be $140 billion, of which $97 billion would accrue to the high-income countries themselves. This is analogous to our multilateral opening simulation, since we remove all barriers only in the industrial countries in our sample. In addition, the countries in our sample account for only about 86 percent of the combined GDP of all industrial economies. Nonetheless, we project that multilateral opening in all eight would raise global incomes by about $550 billion (in 1997 dollars), with developing countries gaining $100 billion. Thus (allowing for inflation between 1995 and 1997) our estimated gains are about four times as large as those of Anderson et al. for the world as a whole, and about six times as large for the industrial (or high-income) countries. This indicates that the potential gains from deeper integration among the industrial countries are far larger than estimates that consider only conventional barriers (as do Anderson et al. 2001) would suggest. Of course, such extensive liberalization in these countries may not be an option because of the short-run political stresses that would be caused by contraction in these countries' protected sectors. Our analysis does not provide a recipe for reform, but it does show that the potential gains from future attempts to integrate markets remain quite large.

Winners and Losers

Although our analysis shows that all the countries examined would gain from further opening to trade, some groups within those countries would lose, while others would win. An examination of real factor price changes sheds light on this issue. The model we use contains five factors: capital, skilled labor, unskilled labor, land, and natural resources. We can therefore obtain broad results on income distribution among these large groups.

Table 4.2 reports the effects of trade opening on after-tax real factor prices for the different scenarios.

Both types of labor gain in all countries in each scenario, indicating that, for these industrial countries at least, market fragmentation imposes burdens on workers as a whole. The more efficient allocation of resources that opening brings would raise workers' real income overall. Of course, some workers may have to pay the costs of adjusting between sectors in the short run—costs that the model does not capture. Overall, these gains are remarkable but not entirely unexpected, given that the model is not based solely on perfect competition. Whereas traditional models based on the Hecksher-Ohlin framework would lead us to expect that the production factors used relatively intensively in import-competing industries, such as unskilled labor, would lose from liberalization (the Stolper-Samuelson theorem), models that allow for imperfect competition, scale economies, and additional investment can yield more optimistic implications.[3]

Capital benefits from opening as well, except in Australia in the cases of multilateral opening and the eight-country PTA, and in the United States under the PTA. Japanese capital owners would gain quite a bit more than their counterparts in other countries, reflecting the fact that Japan generally has comparative advantage in capital-intensive goods.

These simulations imply huge impacts on landowners in certain countries. In all scenarios involving Japan, the modeling predicts that Japanese landowners' real incomes would decline by nearly half. Indeed, these results may help explain why Japan has been slow to liberalize despite the benefits that it would enjoy in the aggregate. Italian, British, and, to a more moderate degree, German landowners would also be hurt by unilateral opening. On the other hand, Australian, Canadian, and Dutch landowners would reap huge benefits from both multilateral opening and the PTA.[4] These gains would be much higher than with unilateral opening because agricultural protection in these countries is relatively low, meaning that enhanced export opportunities, not cheaper imports, provide the main payoffs. The opening of foreign markets, especially in Japan, combined with free markets in manufactures at home, would increase real returns to land by one third or more in these countries. In the United States, landowners' welfare depends crucially on whether opening is unilateral or multilateral. Whereas unilateral liberalization hurts US landowners, multilateral opening increases the real returns to US land by 6 percent, and a PTA provides a 12 percent boost. The results also indicate

---

3. For a review see Krugman and Obstfeld (2003, chapters 4 and 6).

4. It should be kept in mind that these countries' large shares of trade in GDP amplify the percentage changes.

Table 4.2 Welfare impact on economic factors in sample countries of complete removal of barriers
(percent of income of indicated factor)

Type of opening and factor affected	Australia	Canada	Germany	Italy	Japan	Netherlands	United Kingdom	United States
Worldwide opening by countries individually								
Skilled labor	2.3	3.8	5.2	3.4	7.8	9.1	6.4	1.1
Unskilled labor	2.5	3.8	5.3	3.2	7.0	10.7	6.6	1.1
Capital	0.2	1.3	3.4	1.6	6.8	2.5	1.5	0.4
Land	5.5	3.0	−0.4	−14.0	−47.4	8.5	−6.4	−0.6
Natural resources	9.6	7.7	6.6	0.0	−21.6	14.3	18.9	6.6
Worldwide opening by all eight countries								
Skilled labor	3.2	5.0	5.8	4.0	8.0	11.0	6.9	1.2
Unskilled labor	4.5	5.7	6.1	4.3	7.3	14.2	7.3	1.4
Capital	−0.4	1.1	3.4	1.4	6.9	2.0	1.3	0.0
Land	36.5	38.3	7.4	−7.9	−47.2	33.3	−1.0	6.4
Natural resources	14.5	14.6	10.4	1.8	−21.1	19.7	25.7	11.0
FTA by the eight countries								
Skilled labor	3.0	4.4	3.6	3.2	6.0	8.8	4.1	1.0
Unskilled labor	4.8	5.7	4.1	4.4	5.4	13.6	4.8	1.3
Capital	−0.7	0.5	1.8	0.6	5.0	0.8	0.2	−0.2
Land	49.9	45.0	15.5	2.8	−42.2	74.0	4.5	11.6
Natural resources	−2.5	4.1	4.8	1.5	−13.3	1.8	9.0	1.7

that natural resource owners are heavily protected in Japan. However, natural resource factors are the most difficult to measure, making these results the most uncertain.

Overall, these simulations provide a compelling picture of the potential gains from deeper international integration in industrial countries. They suggest not only that each country will gain in the aggregate, but also that most productive factors within each country will gain. The noteworthy exceptions are owners of land in Italy, Japan, and the United Kingdom and owners of natural resources in Japan. They help explain, too, why the trends toward deeper integration among industrial countries have been so strong over the past half century and why agriculture, particularly in Europe and Japan, has been a noteworthy exception.

Additional Description of the Model and Methodology

Production Structure

Production involves the use of intermediate goods and, as noted above, five factors: capital, skilled labor, unskilled labor, land, and natural resources. In our model only capital can move freely across national boundaries; all factors can move freely across sectors. Value added in each sector has a constant elasticity of substitution (CES) production function. This formulation means that, within each sector, the elasticity of substitution between any two factors is the same. We use the same values as Harrison, Rutherford, and Tarr (1997) for these elasticities, which they estimated using US time-series data from 1947 to 1982 and using the same functional form as we used in our applied general equilibrium model. They, however, used only three factors—capital, labor, and land—instead of five. See table 4.3 for these estimates and their standard errors. The production function for intermediate goods and the value-added composite is that of Leontief. Relaxing this assumption does not significantly change the results.

Some sectors are assumed to have constant returns to scale. Other sectors, however, are modeled with increasing returns to scale and imperfect competition.[5] In these sectors there is firm-level product differentiation, with output being a composite of varieties. Firms have fixed costs and constant marginal costs, meaning that reducing the number of firms leads to gains from rationalization. These firms compete using quantity conjectures, with entry and exit that drive profits to zero.

---

5. See table 4.3 for the sectors and the markups used. The table also presents alternative markups from the GTAP model. The results are robust to the set of markups used.

Table 4.3 Estimated factor substitution elasticities and Lerner indices by sector

Product category	Factor substitution elasticity	Standard error	Lerner indices[a]	
			HRT	GTAP
Fruits, nuts, vegetables	0.945	0.041	0	0
Other agriculture	0.945	0.041	0	0
Other crops	0.945	0.041	0	0
Live animals	0.945	0.041	0	0
Other animal products	0.945	0.041	0	0
Fish	0.945	0.041	0.05	0
Coal, gas, oil	0.293	0.102	0.03	0.05
Other minerals	0.426	0.105	0.08	0.05
Bovine cattle, sheep, goat, and horse products	0.945	0.041	0.10	0
Other meat products	0.945	0.041	0.10	0
Vegetable oils and fats	0.945	0.041	0.03	0
Dairy products	0.945	0.041	0	0
Processed rice	0.945	0.041	0.13	0
Sugar	0.945	0.041	0.03	0
Other food products	0.945	0.041	0.03	0
Beverages and tobacco products	0.945	0.041	0.03	0
Textiles	0.927	0.077	0.06	0.14
Wearing apparel	0.927	0.077	0.13	0.13
Leather goods	0.927	0.077	0.13	0.13
Lumber and wood products	0.945	0.041	0.05	0
Pulp, paper products, publishing	1.202	0.090	0.05	0.15
Coal and petroleum products	0.293	0.102	0.03	0.05
Chemicals, plastics, and rubber	1.009	0.027	0.04	0.15
Nonmetallic mineral products	0.426	0.105	0.08	0.05
Primary ferrous metals	0.911	0.241	0.05	0.13
Nonferrous metals	0.958	0.132	0.05	0.13
Fabricated metal products	1.189	0.055	0.05	0.12
Motor vehicles and parts	1.202	0.090	0.11	0.12
Electronic equipment	1.202	0.090	0.06	0.15
Machinery and equipment	1.202	0.090	0.06	0.15
Other manufacturing products	1.202	0.090	0.06	0.15
Trade and transport services	1.283	0.525	0	0
Other services	3.125	0.817	0	0
Investment goods	1.988	0.477	0	0

GTAP = Global Trade Analysis Report, www.gtap.org.
HRT, as estimated by Harrison, Rutherford, and Tarr (1997).

a. Defined as $(P - MC)/P$, where P is price and MC is marginal cost.

Dynamics are incorporated by allowing the capital stock to vary in response to changes in the rate of return caused by liberalization. If the rate of return increases, investment increases the capital stock until its return is driven back down to the long-run equilibrium. The results, therefore, reflect the model's predictions for what happens after the capital stock has changed by enough to return the price of capital to its original level. The capital adjustment process is not modeled, and the time horizon implied by these results depends on how long one thinks it takes capital to respond to differences in interest rates. The model ignores the consumption forgone by the increased investment, which may overstate the estimated benefits. On the other hand, the model ignores any impact of growth on productivity and innovation, which leads to an underestimate of the gains.

Demand Structure

On the demand side, each region has a representative consumer and a single government agent, each of whom has a nested CES utility function and practices multistage budgeting. At the top level, demand across the 33 sectors is Cobb-Douglas. Consumers first decide how much to spend on each of the 33 aggregate goods, given total income and aggregate prices. Each of these goods is a CES composite of domestic output and an import composite, which are imperfect substitutes. At this second level, consumers divide spending between the domestic good and the import by maximizing a CES utility function subject to the total spending they have allocated to that sector and given the aggregate prices in that sector. At the third level, the model invokes the Armington assumption in that imports of the same good from different countries are assumed to be imperfect substitutes. Preferences across these different goods from different countries are given by a CES utility function. At this third level, consumers choose quantities of each import subject to the amount they have budgeted for aggregate imports at the second level and subject to the various prices. We follow Harrison, Rutherford, and Tarr (1997) and set the elasticity of substitution across import varieties, σ_{MM}, equal to 8 and the elasticity of substitution between the import composite and the domestic good, σ_{DM}, equal to 4. The choice of these elasticities does affect the results. Higher elasticities lead to greater substitution in response to price reductions and, in general, larger welfare gains from liberalization. Roughly speaking, cutting these elasticities in half reduces the gains by 10 to 50 percent, depending on the region and the simulation. Similarly, doubling them increases the estimated gains by about 20 to 100 percent. Even such wide changes in the calibration, however, do not change any of our main conclusions.[6]

In the sectors with increasing returns, yet another level of constrained choice is introduced. In this setup the domestic good and each import good produced in each region, instead of being homogeneous goods, are themselves composites of different varieties produced by the different firms. Consumers have CES preferences over these varieties and allocate spending across them subject to the amount they budgeted

---

6. Recent studies indicate that elasticities of 8 and 4 are perhaps on the low side, indicating that our predicted gains are conservative.

for each good at the third level. The elasticity of substitution across these varieties is set at 15. All results are robust to wide changes in this parameter.

Incorporating Our New Data

In the original model, all policy distortions enter as ad valorem price wedges,[7] which, conveniently, is the form that our protection data take. So replacing the GTAP tariff equivalents with our own is fairly straightforward. We did not, however, simply use our fragmentation measures, since they apply only to final goods, whereas almost all of the sectors of the model contain a combination of final and intermediate goods. Instead we used a weighted average of our data (BL) and the original GTAP data. The weight on our measure was the fraction of output in that sector sold to final demand; the weight on the GTAP measure was 1 minus our weight. Thus, letting BL and GTAP be the two protection measures, and α the final demand fraction, the protection estimate used was αBL + (1 − α)GTAP. Using this method ensures that model sectors with a high proportion of final goods use an estimate of protection close to ours, whereas sectors with a low fraction of final goods use an estimate close to the GTAP measure. Put another way, the lower the final demand fraction, the less we deviated from the standard GTAP data. See table 4.4 for a comparison of these weighted data and the original GTAP data.

The data on distribution margins used to derive the protection measures allow us to model distribution more accurately within the applied general equilibrium (AGE) framework. Most AGE trade models using this framework do not account for margins explicitly. All distribution services are lumped into the trade and transport sector and consumed as a separate good, instead of being linked to the goods that use those distribution services. Since margins vary across sectors, this obscures the role of distribution in the economy and can skew the results of applied general equilibrium analyses. For instance, simulations of price reductions in other sectors may imply a large substitution out of trade and transport services, even though actual consumption of these services would probably increase in order to facilitate commodity flows. Also, not accounting for margins implies that consumers base their choices on producer prices instead of the higher consumer prices, which include margins.

We attempt to address these problems by incorporating distribution explicitly into each final demand sector for which we have data on margins. We do this by treating margins like taxes, since margins create a wedge between consumer and producer prices. For the eight countries

---

7. Government revenue is held constant throughout all simulations by assuming that lump-sum taxes are enacted to replace any lost tax revenue.

Table 4.4 Comparison of weighted data and original GTAP data

Product category	Australia	Canada	Germany	Italy	Japan	Netherlands	United Kingdom	United States
New data[a]								
Fruits, nuts, and vegetables	4.6	6.0	35.1	15.3	94.1	13.9	34.0	17.4
Other agriculture								
Other crops	2.1	66.8	83.0	6.9	52.5	9.7	89.1	32.2
Live animals	1.0	0.3	36.6	31.4	149.1	34.9	38.2	1.1
Other animal products	7.2	19.3	6.7	6.4	7.8	7.2	25.6	2.3
Fish	8.6	1.2	11.4	11.4	16.2	8.7	7.7	5.1
Coal, gas, oil								
Other minerals								
Bovine cattle, sheep, goat, and horse products	0.0	18.1	109.7	39.0	265.4	80.6	99.6	8.3
Other meat products	3.0	29.3	41.8	23.3	119.8	29.6	37.6	5.5
Vegetable oils and fats	20.2	13.1	27.3	15.4	46.0	13.8	12.2	6.0
Dairy products	19.1	77.8	30.8	33.8	173.7	53.0	43.4	32.0
Processed rice	0.4	0.6	47.9	28.9	224.3	25.4	23.7	13.1
Sugar	11.7	8.3	66.3	37.2	111.0	72.4	69.2	46.9
Other food products	10.9	11.4	21.5	24.8	98.3	23.8	27.1	11.3
Beverages and tobacco products	54.1	35.6	33.9	37.8	59.6	35.2	45.2	15.4
Textiles	24.9	26.3	30.1	9.4	16.6	29.8	29.9	16.8
Wearing apparel	12.7	24.2	23.1	46.1	33.4	33.5	26.0	14.0
Leather goods	27.9	22.8	27.5	12.2	71.4	84.1	20.9	14.1
Lumber and wood products	5.7	8.4	4.2	4.4	4.6	6.2	8.8	2.6
Pulp, paper products, publishing	3.9	5.6	3.2	4.2	4.7	12.7	5.7	2.3
Coal and petroleum products								
Chemicals, plastics, and rubber	4.0	5.4	8.7	5.7	7.6	5.7	7.4	10.4
Nonmetallic mineral products	6.0	13.4	8.6	5.3	10.8	7.3	8.2	6.8
Primary ferrous metals								
Nonferrous metals								
Fabricated metal products	6.6	6.5	3.7	4.2	3.5	5.6	5.9	4.6
Motor vehicles and parts	11.4	6.7	11.1	9.7	0.1	20.1	27.9	7.8
Electronic equipment	3.4	10.6	5.7	5.6	5.9	4.9	8.5	2.4
Machinery and equipment	7.2	4.1	4.7	3.7	2.6	4.4	9.7	4.2
Other manufacturing products	10.3	9.3	10.7	5.1	18.7	21.8	11.9	5.7
Trade and transport services								
Other services								
Investment goods								

GTAP data

Fruits, nuts, vegetables	2.0	1.9	14.5	14.5	44.9	14.5	14.5	4.7
Other agriculture	1.0	2.0	3.0	18.0	30.0	4.5	23.0	3.0
Other crops	2.7	2.4	3.1	3.1	22.1	3.1	3.1	21.5
Live animals	0.8	0.2	36.6	36.6	149.1	36.6	36.6	1.1
Other animal products	0.5	19.8	6.7	6.7	5.0	6.7	6.7	0.6
Fish	0.3	0.4	6.8	9.6	4.9	7.5	6.9	0.6
Coal, gas, oil	0.0	0.0	0.0	0.0	-0.8	0.0	0.0	0.2
Other minerals	0.1	0.0	0.0	0.0	0.0	0.0	0.0	0.4
Bovine cattle, sheep, goat, and horse products	0.1	16.3	88.9	88.9	36.4	88.9	88.9	5.3
Other meat products	4.1	72.4	30.9	30.9	58.2	30.9	30.9	3.6
Vegetable oils and fats	2.8	8.6	11.4	11.4	6.6	11.4	11.4	4.3
Dairy products	7.3	214.8	87.7	87.7	287.0	87.7	87.7	42.5
Processed rice	1.0	0.7	87.4	87.4	409.0	87.4	87.4	5.3
Sugar	13.9	4.9	76.4	76.4	116.1	76.4	76.4	53.4
Other food products	5.6	14.1	28.8	28.8	38.3	28.8	28.8	11.4
Beverages and tobacco products	9.2	62.5	8.3	8.3	16.2	8.3	8.3	3.0
Textiles	17.0	15.7	9.7	9.2	8.5	9.8	9.5	11.2
Wearing apparel	29.3	21.2	12.1	12.2	12.5	12.0	11.9	13.3
Leather goods	13.0	15.3	8.4	6.5	15.3	8.7	8.7	13.5
Lumber and wood products	4.5	6.8	2.8	2.7	2.7	3.0	2.8	2.2
Pulp, paper products, publishing	3.1	1.9	2.9	2.4	0.5	2.7	2.6	1.0
Coal and petroleum products	0.0	6.2	2.7	3.0	3.3	3.1	2.9	2.2
Chemicals, plastics, and rubber	3.5	4.8	5.1	5.3	2.0	4.8	4.7	3.5
Nonmetallic mineral products	4.7	5.7	5.4	5.2	1.2	5.2	5.1	6.1
Primary ferrous metals	4.7	4.7	3.2	3.2	2.5	3.2	3.4	3.4
Nonferrous metals	1.4	0.5	2.1	1.2	0.4	2.9	1.5	1.7
Fabricated metal products	6.4	6.3	3.7	3.9	1.2	4.0	3.8	3.8
Motor vehicles and parts	9.2	6.1	7.7	8.6	0.0	8.4	8.3	2.4
Electronic equipment	1.6	1.2	4.3	4.5	0.0	4.2	4.2	1.2
Machinery and equipment	4.3	3.3	3.1	3.1	0.3	3.1	3.1	2.7
Other manufacturing products	3.7	3.8	3.7	3.8	1.9	3.9	2.5	1.7
Trade and transport services	0.0	0.0	0.0	0.0	0.0	0.0	0.0	0.0
Other services	0.0	0.0	0.0	0.0	0.0	0.0	0.0	0.0
Investment goods	0.0	0.0	0.0	0.0	0.0	0.0	0.0	0.0

GTAP = Global Trade Analysis Project data, www.gtap.org.

a. Weighted averages of authors' final goods protection data and GTAP data, with the final demand fraction in each sector used as the weight. Sectors for which the authors' protection data did not apply are left blank.

involved, therefore, we inserted margin wedges into each of the relevant sectors.[8] We also reduced the value of the trade and transport sector by the total value of these margins. Finally, we reduced inputs into the trade and transport sector and redistributed them across the final goods sectors in accordance with the amount of distribution services used in those sectors.[9]

8. See Gohin (1998) and Komen and Peerlings (1996) for other examples of modeling margins in this way within applied general equilibrium models. Bradford and Gohin (2002) explicitly model the distribution sector for the United States within such a model.

9. These modifications apply only to final goods. Because of lack of data, we do not modify the model to account for distribution of intermediate goods. It turns out that these intermediate margins are quite a bit smaller than the margins for final goods.

Appendix 4.1
Confidence Intervals

Most researchers using applied general equilibrium models report only point estimates for their simulations and then check the robustness of their results by varying influential parameters in systematic but somewhat ad hoc ways. Abdelkhalek and Dufour (1998), however, present a straightforward procedure for developing well-grounded confidence intervals for these simulations. They point out that when simulation parameters are estimated and therefore have standard errors, one can derive confidence intervals for endogenous variables by using a projection technique. This involves using the standard errors for the estimated parameters to set appropriate lower and upper bounds.

Let $\hat{\beta}_i$ be one of k estimated model parameters. Invoking the Boole-Benferroni inequality, Abdelkhalek and Dufour show that the lower bound of a $1 - \alpha$ confidence interval for an endogenous variable can be found by setting all the estimated parameters equal to the lower bound of a $1 - \alpha/k$ confidence interval. Thus, if s_i is the standard error for $\hat{\beta}_i$ and is normally distributed, then the value of this parameter inserted into the model in order to get a lower bound is $\hat{\beta}_i - z_{\alpha/k}s_i$ (where z refers to a critical value from the standard normal distribution). This is done for all k parameters. Similarly, using $\hat{\beta}_i + z_{\alpha/k}s_i$ for each of the k parameters produces the upper bound. These confidence intervals will be conservative (that is, probably wider than needed), because this approach assumes that each of the parameter estimates is independent of each of the others. If some or all of the covariance structure across the parameter estimates is known, one could exploit that knowledge to derive tighter intervals (Abdelkhalek and Dufour 1998).

As discussed in the text, the only parameters that influence our results, besides σ_{MM} and σ_{DM}, are the factor substitution elasticities. Since these parameters are estimated, we can use their point estimates and standard errors to derive confidence intervals for our welfare results. Table 4.3 presents the substitution elasticity estimates, along with their standard errors. There are 12 different estimates, and so the lower bound of a 95 percent confidence interval on the simulation results will result from replacing each of these estimates with $\hat{\beta}_i - z_{0.05/12}s_i = \hat{\beta}_i - 2.64s_i$. The upper bound will be found by using $\hat{\beta}_i + 2.64s_i$ instead. Table A4.1 reports the upper and lower bounds for these 95 percent confidence intervals for overall welfare changes.[10] For all of the main results (those on the diagonal), the gains are positive with 95 percent confidence and are almost certainly large.

To be sure, these confidence intervals are conditional on the model and the other parameters (the ones that are not varied) being correct. Any

---

10. It turns out that the confidence intervals for factor prices are extremely small, so they are not reported.

Table A4.1 Upper and lower bounds on confidence intervals for welfare estimates

Country or countries removing barriers

Country or region affected	Australia		Canada		Germany		Italy		Japan		Netherlands		United Kingdom		United States		All eight countries		Eight-country FTA	
	Low	High	Low	High	Low	High	Low	High	Low	High	Low	High	Low	High	Low	High	Low	High	Low	High
Australia	0.67	2.51	0.01	0.03	0.05	0.17	0.01	0.04	0.99	2.31	0.00	0.02	0.14	0.35	0.15	0.39	2.02	5.89	2.37	6.29
Canada	0.02	0.06	0.16	1.80	0.02	0.06	0.08	0.12	0.32	0.72	0.01	0.02	0.04	0.11	1.26	2.16	1.86	5.15	1.93	5.39
Germany	0.01	0.04	−0.01	−0.01	0.47	2.04	0.17	0.32	−0.12	0.03	0.20	0.40	0.16	0.45	0.06	0.19	0.99	3.59	0.94	2.98
Italy	0.02	0.07	0.01	0.04	0.36	0.98	0.85	2.98	−0.09	0.14	0.06	0.17	0.17	0.60	0.07	0.26	1.51	5.42	2.36	6.78
Japan	0.03	0.06	−0.01	0.00	−0.02	0.00	0.00	0.01	2.92	3.19	0.01	0.02	−0.01	0.02	0.09	0.16	3.05	3.50	1.98	2.37
Netherlands	0.03	0.07	0.00	0.01	1.12	1.97	0.46	0.70	−0.03	0.29	1.37	6.03	0.66	1.41	0.22	0.42	3.77	11.59	5.58	13.00
United Kingdom	0.01	0.00	0.01	0.02	0.16	0.38	0.07	0.13	0.17	0.30	0.14	0.29	1.54	4.88	0.13	0.28	2.23	6.47	1.34	4.29
United States	0.00	−0.02	0.13	0.28	0.02	0.06	0.01	0.01	0.29	0.52	0.01	0.02	0.04	0.09	0.16	0.65	0.53	1.55	0.88	1.85
China	0.03	0.06	0.04	0.06	0.10	0.14	0.03	0.05	0.72	0.83	0.01	0.04	0.04	0.08	0.51	0.58	1.35	1.62	−0.62	−0.53
Korea	0.03	0.04	0.00	0.00	0.02	0.04	0.01	0.01	0.53	0.69	0.00	0.00	0.01	0.05	0.20	0.29	0.78	1.14	−0.49	−0.51
Rest of Asia	0.04	0.09	0.01	0.04	0.12	0.27	0.04	0.09	0.66	1.36	0.01	0.07	0.11	0.27	0.31	0.66	1.31	2.74	−0.77	−0.81
Brazil	−0.02	−0.04	0.01	0.02	0.12	0.24	0.03	0.09	0.34	0.50	0.01	0.04	0.06	0.13	0.21	0.43	0.77	1.36	0.10	−0.07
Rest of Latin America	0.00	−0.01	−0.01	−0.01	0.09	0.22	0.04	0.10	0.34	0.75	0.02	0.03	0.06	0.13	0.53	1.18	1.19	2.70	−0.35	−0.62
Rest of Europe	0.01	0.03	0.00	0.01	0.35	0.83	0.12	0.28	0.03	0.22	0.10	0.27	0.27	0.68	0.08	0.22	0.95	2.50	−0.71	−0.96
Middle East	0.01	0.00	0.02	0.03	0.20	0.49	0.10	0.22	0.40	0.72	0.06	0.13	0.23	0.51	0.29	0.53	1.32	2.67	−0.03	0.03
Rest of world	−0.01	−0.01	0.00	0.02	0.24	0.49	0.11	0.21	0.36	0.53	0.05	0.09	0.14	0.29	0.07	0.15	0.99	1.76	0.10	0.02
Developing countries	0.02	0.02	0.01	0.03	0.15	0.30	0.06	0.13	0.48	0.80	0.03	0.07	0.10	0.22	0.30	0.56	1.14	2.11	−0.29	−0.37
Industrial countries	0.02	0.07	0.05	0.16	0.14	0.44	0.09	0.26	0.78	1.03	0.07	0.21	0.18	0.54	0.15	0.43	1.45	3.13	1.13	2.42
World	0.02	0.06	0.04	0.13	0.14	0.40	0.08	0.22	0.70	0.97	0.06	0.17	0.16	0.46	0.18	0.46	1.37	2.88	0.78	1.74

confidence interval is conditional on the underlying model being correct, and so this aspect of our confidence intervals does not distinguish them from conventional ones. In addition, however, our confidence intervals depend on the value of any influential fixed parameters, such as the elasticity of substitution between domestic goods and the corresponding import composites, σ_{DM}, and the elasticity of substitution across import varieties, σ_{MM}. As mentioned in the text, varying these parameters widely by halving or doubling them does affect the magnitude of the welfare gains but does not affect whether any confidence interval lies entirely above zero. Thus the main story told by the interval estimates is robust to wide changes in other parameters.

References

Abdelkhalek, T., and J.-M. Dufour. 1998. Statistical Inference for Computable General Equilibrium Models, with Application to a Model of the Moroccan Economy. *Review of Economics and Statistics* 80 (November): 520–34.

Anderson, James E., and Eric van Wincoop. 2002. Borders, Trade and Welfare. In *Brookings Trade Forum 2001*, ed. Susan M. Collins and Dani Rodrik. Washington: Brookings Institution.

Anderson, James E., and Eric van Wincoop. 2003. Gravity with Gravitas: A Solution to the Border Puzzle. *American Economic Review* 93, no. 1: 170–92.

Anderson, Kym, Betina Dimaranan, Joe Francois, Tom Hertel, Bernard Hoekman, and Will Martin. 2001. *The Cost of Rich (and Poor) Country Protection to Developing Countries*. Adelaide, South Australia: Adelaide University.

Bergsten, C. Fred, and Marcus Noland. 1993. *Reconcilable Differences? United States Japan Economic Conflict*. Washington: Institute for International Economics.

Bergsten, C. Fred, Taketoshi Ito, and Marcus Noland. 2001. *No More Bashing: Building a New Japan-United States Economic Relationship*. Washington: Institute for International Economics.

Bhagwati, J. 1991. *The World Trading System at Risk*. Princeton: Princeton University.

Bhagwati, J., and R. E. Hudec, eds. 1996. *Fair Trade and Harmonization: Prerequisites for Free Trade?* Cambridge, MA: MIT Press.

Bradford, Scott. 2002. The Welfare Effects of Distribution Regulations in OECD Countries. Brigham Young University. Photocopy.

Bradford, Scott. 2003a. Paying the Price: Final Good Protection in OECD Countries. *Review of Economics and Statistics* 85, no. 1: 24–37.

Bradford, Scott. 2003b. Rejuvenating Japan: Potential Gains from Deregulating International Trade and Domestic Distribution. Brigham Young University. Photocopy.

Bradford, Scott, and Alex Gohin. 2002. Modeling Distribution Services and Assessing Their Welfare Effects in a General Equilibrium Framework. Brigham Young University and Institut National de la Recherche Agronomique, Paris. Photocopy.

Cecchetti, Stephen G., C. Mark Nelson, and Robert J. Sonora. 2002. Price Index Convergence Among United States Cities. *International Economic Review* 43, no. 4: 1081–99.

Crucini, Mario, Chris Telmer, and Marios Zachariadis. 2000. *Dispersion in Real Exchange Rates*. Philadelphia: University of Pennsylvania.

Crucini, Mario, Chris Telmer, and Marios Zachariadis. 2001. *Understanding European Real Exchange Rates*. Philadelphia: University of Pennsylvania.

Deardorff, Alan, and Robet Stern. 1998. *Measurement of Non-tariff Barriers*. Ann Arbor, MI: University of Michigan Press.

Emerson, Michael, Michel Aujean, Michel Catinat, et al. 1988. *The Economics of 1992: The E.C. Commission's Assessment of the Economic Effects of Completing the Internal Market*. Oxford, UK: Oxford University Press.

Engel, Charles, and John H. Rogers. 1996. How Wide Is the Border? *American Economic Review* 86, no. 5: 1112–25.

Engel, Charles, and John H. Rogers. 1997. Regional Patterns in the Law of One Price. In *The Regionalization of the World Economy*, ed. Jeffrey A. Frankel. Chicago: University of Chicago Press.

Engel, Charles, and John H. Rogers. 1999. *Violating the Law of One Price: Should We Make a Federal Case Out of It?* NBER Working Paper 7242. Cambridge, MA: National Bureau of Economic Research.

Engel, Charles, and John H. Rogers. 2000. Relative Price Volatility: What Role Does the Border Play? in *International Macroeconomics*, ed. Gregory Hess and Eric van Wincoop. Cambridge: Cambridge University Press.

European Central Bank. 2002. Price Level Convergence and Competition in the Euro Area. *Monthly Bulletin* (August): 39–50.

European Commission, Directorate-General for Economic and Financial Affairs. 2001. *Price Levels and Price Dispersion in the EU*. Brussels: European Commission.

Eurostat-OECD PPP Programme. 1996. *The Calculation and Aggregation of Parities*. Brussels: OECD.

Evans, Carolyn. 1998. Do National Border Effects Matter? Cambridge, MA: Economics Department, Harvard University.

Evans, Carolyn. 2001. *Home Bias in Trade: Location or Foreign-ness?* New York: Federal Reserve Bank of New York.

Feenstra, Robert C., James A. Markusen, and Andrew K. Rose. 1998. *Undertstanding the Home Market Effect and the Gravity Equation: The Role of Differentiating Goods*. NBER Working Paper 6804. Cambridge, MA: National Bureau of Economic Research.

Frankel, Jeffrey A. 1997. *Regional Trading Blocs in the World Economic System*. Washington: Institute for International Economics.

Frankel, Jeffrey, and Andrew Rose. 2002. An Estimate of the Effect of Common Currencies on Trade and Income. *Quarterly Journal of Economics* 117, no. 2: 437–66.

Froot, Kenneth, Michael Kim, and Kenneth Rogoff. 1995. *The Law of One Price over 700 Years*. NBER Working Paper 5132. Cambridge, MA: National Bureau of Economic Research.

Giovannini, Alberto. 1988. Exchange Rates and Traded Goods Prices. *Journal of International Economics* 24: 45–68.

Gohin, Alexandre. 1998. Modelisation du complexe agro-alimentaire français dans un cadre d'equilibre general. Ph.D. thesis, Université de Paris I. Pantheon-Sorbonne.

Goldberg, Pinelopi K., and Frank Verboven. 2001. *Market Integration and Convergence to the Law of One Price: Evidence from the European Car Market*. NBER Working Paper 8402. Cambridge, MA: National Bureau of Economic Research.

Goto, Fumihiro. 1990. Is the Japanese Market Really Closed? A Critical Review of the Economic Studies. Research Institute of International Trade and Industry, Tokyo. Photocopy.

Harrison, G. W., T. F. Rutherford, and D. Tarr. 1995. Quantifying the Outcome of the Uruguay Round. *Finance & Development* 32, no. 4 (December): 38–41.

Harrison, G. W., T. F. Rutherford, and D. Tarr. 1996. Quantifying the Uruguay Round. In *The Uruguay Round and the Developing Countries*, ed. W. Martin and L. A. Winters. New York: Cambridge University Press.

Harrison, G. W., T. F. Rutherford, and D. Tarr. 1997. Quantifying the Uruguay Round. *Economic Journal* 107 (September): 1405–30.

Haskal, Jonathan, and Holger Wolf. 2001. *The Law of One Price—A Case Study*. NBER Working Paper 8112. Cambridge, MA: National Bureau of Economic Research.

Head, Keith, and Thierry Mayer. 1999. Non-Europe: The Magnitude and Causes of Market Fragmentation in the EU. *Weltwirtschaftliches Archiv* 136, no. 2: 284–314.

Head, Keith, and John Ries. 1997. Market-Access Effects of Trade Liberalization: Evidence from the Canada-U.S. Free Trade Agreement. In *The Effects of U.S. Trade Protection and Promotion Policies*, ed. R. Feenstra. Chicago: University of Chicago Press.

Helliwell, John. 1997. *National Borders, Trade and Migration*. NBER Working Paper 6027. Cambridge, MA: National Bureau of Economic Research.

Helliwell, John. 1998. *How Much Do National Borders Matter?* Washington: Brookings Institution.

Holzman, Frank D. 1969. Comparison of Different Forms of Trade Barriers. *Review of Economics and Statistics* 51, no. 2: 159–65.

Hufbauer, Gary Clyde, and Kimberly Ann Elliott. 1994. *Measuring the Costs of Protection in the United States*. Washington: Institute for International Economics.

Hufbauer, Gary Clyde, Erika Wada, and Tony Warren. 2002. *The Benefits of Price Convergence: Speculative Calculations*. POLICY ANALYSES IN INTERNATIONAL ECONOMICS 65. Washington: Institute for International Economics.

Hummels, David, and Alexandre Skiba. 2002. *Shipping the Good Apples Out? An Empirical Confirmation of the Alchian-Allen Conjecture*. NBER Working Paper 9023. Cambridge, MA: National Bureau of Economic Research.

Isard, Peter. 1977. How Far Can We Push the Law of One Price? *American Economic Review* 67: 942–48.

Ito, Takatoshi. 1992. *The Japanese Economy*. Cambridge, MA: MIT Press.

Kim, Namdoo. 1996. *Measuring the Costs of Visible Protection in Korea*. Washington: Institute for International Economics.

Knetter, Michael M. 1989. Price Discrimination by US and German Exporters. *American Economic Review* 79, no. 1: 198–210.

Knetter, Michael M., and Pinelopi K. Goldberg. 1995. *Measuring the Intensity of Competition in Export Markets*. NBER Working Paper 5226. Cambridge, MA: National Bureau of Economic Research.

Knetter, Michael M., and Pinelopi K. Goldberg. 1996. *Goods Prices and Exchange Rates: What Have We Learned?* NBER Working Paper 5862. Cambridge, MA: National Bureau of Economic Research.

Knetter, Michael M., and Matthew J. Slaughter. 1999. *Measuring Product-Market Integration*. NBER Working Paper 6969. Cambridge, MA: National Bureau of Economic Research.

Komen, M. H. C, and J. H. M. Peerlings. 1996. WAGEM: An Applied General Equilibrium Model for Agricultural and Environmental Policy Analysis. Wageningen Economic Papers 1996-4. The Netherlands: Wageningen University.

Krugman, Paul R. 1990. *The Age of Diminished Expectations: U.S. Economic Policy in the 1990s*. Cambridge, MA: MIT Press.

Krugman, Paul R. 1997. What Should Trade Negotiators Negotiate About? *Journal of Economic Literature* 35 (March): 113–20.

Krugman, Paul R., and Maurice Obstfeld. 2003. *International Economics: Theory and Policy*. Boston: Addison Wesley.

Lawrence, Robert Z. 1979. Within- and Between-Country Variances in Inflation Rates: Are They Similar? *Journal of Monetary Economics* 5, no. 1: 145–52.

Lawrence, Robert Z. 1987. Does Japan Import Too Little: Closed Markets or Minds? *Brookings Papers on Economic Activity* 2: 517–54.

Lawrence, Robert Z. 1991. Efficient or Exclusionist? The Import Behavior of Japanese Corporate Groups. *Brookings Papers on Economic Activity* 1: 311–30.

Lawrence, Robert Z. 1993. Japan's Different Trade Regime: An Analysis with Particular Reference to Keiretsu. *Journal of Economic Perspectives* 7, no. 3: 3–19.

Lawrence, Robert Z., Albert Bressand, and Takatoshi Ito. 1996. *A Vision for the World Economy: Openness, Diversity and Cohesion.* Washington: Brookings Institution.

Leamer, Edward. 1984. *Sources of International Comparative Advantage.* Cambridge, MA: MIT Press.

Lutz, Matthias. 2002. *Price Convergence Under EMU? First Estimates.* St. Gallen, Switzerland: University of St. Gallen.

Malueg, David A., and Marius Schwartz. 1994. Parallel Imports, Demand Dispersion and International Price Discrimination. *Journal of International Economics* 37: 167–96.

Marston, Richard. 1990. Pricing to Market in Japanese Manufacturing. *Journal of International Economics* 29: 217–36.

Maskus, Keith E. 2000. *Intellectual Property Rights in the Global Economy.* Washington: Institute for International Economics.

McCallum, John. 1995. National Borders Matter: Regional Trade Patterns in North America. *American Economic Review* 85, no. 3: 615–23.

Messerlin, Patrick A. 2001. *Measuring the Costs of Protection in Europe: European Commercial Policy in the 2000s.* Washington: Institute for International Economics.

Noland, Marcus. 1995. Why Are Prices So High in Japan? *Japan and the World Economy* 7: 255–61.

Noland, Marcus. 1997. Public Policy, Private Preferences, and the Japanese Trade Pattern. *Review of Economics and Statistics* 79, no. 2: 259–66.

Obstfeld, Maurice, and Kenneth Rogoff. 2000. The Six Major Puzzles in International Macroeconomics: Is There a Common Cause? In *NBER Macroeconomics Annual 2000*, ed. Ben S. Bernanke and Julio Rotemberg. Cambridge, MA: National Bureau of Economic Research.

O'Connell, Paul, and Shang-Jin Wei. 2002. The Bigger They Are, the Harder They Fall: How Are Price Differences Across U.S. Cities Arbitraged? *Journal of International Economics* 56, no. 1: 21–53.

OECD (Organization for Economic Cooperation and Development). 1995. *Purchasing Power Parities and Real Expenditure.* Paris: OECD.

Parsley, David C., and Shang-Jin Wei. 1996. Convergence to the Law of One Price Without Trade Barriers or Currency Fluctuations. *Quarterly Journal of Economics* 111: 1211–36.

Parsley, David, and Shang-Jin Wei. 2000. *Explaining the Border Effect: The Role of Exchange Rate Variability, Shipping Costs, and Geography.* NBER Working Paper 7836. Cambridge, MA: National Bureau of Economic Research.

Parsley, David, and Shang-Jin Wei. 2001. *Limiting Currency Volatility to Stimulate Goods Market Integration.* NBER Working Paper 8468. Cambridge, MA: National Bureau of Economic Research.

Richardson, J. David. 1978. Some Empirical Evidence on Commodity Arbitrage and the Law of One Price. *Journal of International Economics* 8, no. 2: 341–51.

Richardson, J. David. 1989. Empirical Research on Trade Liberalization with Imperfect Competition: A Survey. *OECD Economic Studies* 12: 7–50.

Richardson, Martin. 2002. An Elementary Proposition Concerning Parallel Imports. *Journal of International Economics* 56, no. 1: 233–45.

Rogers, John H. 2002. *Monetary Union, Price Level Convergence and Inflation: How Close Is Europe to the United States?* Washington: Board of Governors of the Federal Reserve System.

Rogers, John H., Gary Clyde Hufbauer, and Erika Wada. 2001. *Price Level Convergence and Inflation in Europe.* Institute for International Economics Working Paper WP01-1. Washington: Institute for International Economics.

Rogers, John H., and Hayden P. Smith. 2001. *Border Effects Within the NAFTA Countries.* Washington: Board of Governors of the Federal Reserve System.

Rogoff, Kenneth. 1996. The Purchasing Power Parity Puzzle. *Journal of Economic Literature* 34: 647–68.

Roningen, Vernon, and Alexander Yeats. 1976. Nontariff Distortions of International Trade: Some Preliminary Empirical Evidence. *Weltwirtschaftliches Archiv* 112, no. 4: 613–25.

Rose, Andrew K., and Charles Engel. 2000. *Currency Unions and International Integration.* NBER Working Paper 7872. Cambridge, MA: National Bureau of Economic Research.

Rousslang, Don J., and Theodore To. 1993. Domestic Trade and Transportation Costs as Barriers to International Trade. *Canadian Journal of Economics* 26, no. 1: 208–21.

Saxonhouse, Gary R. 1983. The Micro- and Macroeconomics of Foreign Sales to Japan. In *Trade Policies in the 1980s,* ed. William R. Cline. Washington: Institute for International Economics.

Saxonhouse, Gary R. 1989. Differentiated Products, Economies of Scale, and Access to the Japanese Market. In *Trade Policies for International Competiveness,* ed. R. Feenstra. Chicago: University of Chicago Press.

Saxonhouse, Gary R. 1993. What Does Japanese Trade Structure Tell Us About Japanese Trade Policy? *Journal of Economic Perspectives* 7, no. 3: 21–44.

Sazanami, Yoko, Shujiro Urata, and Hiroki Kawai. 1995. *Measuring the Costs of Protection in Japan.* Washington: Institute for International Economics.

Tirole, Jean. 1989. *The Theory of Industrial Organization.* Cambridge, MA: MIT Press.

Trefler, Daniel. 2001. *The Long and Short of the Canada-U.S. Free Trade Agreement.* NBER Working Paper 8293. Cambridge, MA: National Bureau of Economic Research.

United Nations Conference on Trade and Development. 1992. *Analytical Report by the UNCTAD Secretariat to the Conference.* New York: United Nations.

US Department of Commerce. 1991. Results of the 1991 DOC/MITI Price Survey. US Department of Commerce News.

US International Trade Commission. 1999. *The Economic Effects of Significant US Import Restraints: Second Update 1999.* Washington: US International Trade Commission.

Waterson, Michael. 1984. *Economic Theory of the Industry.* Cambridge, MA: Cambridge University Press.

Wei, Shang-Jin. 1996. *Intra-national Versus International Trade: How Stubborn Are Nations in Global Integration?* NBER Working Paper 5531. Cambridge, MA: National Bureau of Economic Research.

World Bank. 1993. *Purchasing Power of Currencies: Comparing National Incomes Using ICP Data.* Washington: World Bank.

Yager, Loren. 1991. *Price Comparisons Between the Japanese and US Markets.* RAND N-337-CUSJR. Santa Monica, CA: RAND.

Zhang, Shuguang, Yansheng Zhang, and Zhongxin Wan. 1998. *Measuring the Costs of Protection in China.* Washington: Institute for International Economics.

Index

textiles. *See also* products
  quotas, 19
trade agreement, 57–58
  negotiation, 2
  preferential trade agreement, 2, 63,
    64–65
trade barriers. *See also* border effects
  determination of, 11–12
  labor-intensive goods, 19
  measurement approaches
    direct measures, 19
    explicit measures, 18
    in general, 17–19
    gravity equations, 18
    price differentials, 18
    price evidence, 21–24
    quantity approach, 18
    quantity evidence, 19–21
  welfare effects, 21, 25–26
trademark, 14
transportation costs, 5, 7, 27, 37–38, 53, 54.
    See also border effects

United Kingdom. *See also* Europe
  aggregate integration measures, 6*t*
  consumer prices, 7, 8, 32, 32*t*, 33, 33*t*,
    43, 44*t*–45*t*, 46, 52
  fragmentation index, 39–40, 40*t*
  historical price discrepancy, 22
  producer prices, 36, 36*t*, 37*t*, 43, 44*t*–45*t*
  trade barriers, benefits of elimination,
    26
  welfare effects, 58*f*, 59, 74*t*
    capital benefits, 64, 66
    welfare benefits of eliminating
      fragmentation, 9*t*, 10, 60*t*–61*t*
United States
  aggregate integration measures, 6*t*
  Canada/Mexico integration, 2, 4, 8,
    19–21, 46–49
  consumer prices, 7, 32*t*, 33*t*, 34, 44*t*–45*t*,
    46–49
  fragmentation index, 39–40, 40*t*, 54
  imports, pass-through costs, 22
  integration policies, 2
  parallel imports, 14–15

first-sale doctrine, 15
price convergence, 24, 41, 59
  US-Canada, 49*t*
price dispersion, 41–42
producer prices, 5, 7, 35, 36*t*, 37*t*,
  44*t*–45*t*, 54
tariffs, 19
trade barriers
  benefits of elimination, 26
  deadweight costs, 25
trade deficit, Japan, 3
transportation costs, 37–38
welfare effects, 58*f*, 59, 62, 74*t*
  capital benefits, 64
  welfare benefits of eliminating
    fragmentation, 9–10, 9*t*, 60*t*–61*t*
Uruguay Round, 2, 63

welfare effects
  analysis, 57–63
  confidence intervals, 73–75, 74*t*
  determination basis, 5–6
  Does Price Equalization Improve
    Welfare?, 13–15
  in general, 9–10, 57
  model and methodology
    demand structure, 68–69
    new data, 69–72
    production structure, 66–68
    trade barriers elimination, 18–19, 21,
      25–26, 54–55
  welfare benefits of eliminating
    fragmentation, 9–10, 9*t*
  winners and losers, 63–66
workplace concerns, 2
world
  trade barriers, deadweight costs, 25
  welfare effects, 58*f*, 59, 63, 65*t*, 74*t*
    welfare benefits of eliminating
      fragmentation, 9–10, 9*t*, 60*t*–61*t*
World Trade Organization (WTO)
  Doha Round, 1, 2
  Uruguay Round, 2, 63
WTO. *See* World Trade Organization

yen, 53–54

WORKS IN PROGRESS

DISTRIBUTORS OUTSIDE THE UNITED STATES

**Australia, New Zealand,
and Papua New Guinea**
D.A. Information Services
648 Whitehorse Road
Mitcham, Victoria 3132, Australia
tel: 61-3-9210-7777
fax: 61-3-9210-7788
email: service@adadirect.com.au
http://www.dadirect.com.au

United Kingdom and Europe
(including Russia and Turkey)
The Eurospan Group
3 Henrietta Street, Covent Garden
London WC2E 8LU England
tel: 44-20-7240-0856
fax: 44-20-7379-0609
http://www.eurospan.co.uk

Japan and the Republic of Korea
United Publishers Services, Ltd.
KenkyuSha Bldg.
9, Kanda Surugadai 2-Chome
Chiyoda-Ku, Tokyo 101 Japan
tel: 81-3-3291-4541
fax: 81-3-3292-8610
email: saito@ups.co.jp
**For trade accounts only.
Individuals will find IIE books in
leading Tokyo bookstores.**

Thailand
Asia Books
5 Sukhumvit Rd. Soi 61
Bangkok 10110 Thailand
tel: 662-714-07402 Ext: 221, 222, 223
fax: 662-391-2277
email: purchase@asiabooks.co.th
http://www.asiabooksonline.com

Canada
Renouf Bookstore
5369 Canotek Road, Unit 1
Ottawa, Ontario KlJ 9J3, Canada
tel: 613-745-2665
fax: 613-745-7660
http://www.renoufbooks.com

India, Bangladesh, Nepal, and Sri Lanka
Viva Books Pvt.
Mr. Vinod Vasishtha
4325/3, Ansari Rd.
Daryaganj, New Delhi-110002
India
tel: 91-11-327-9280
fax: 91-11-326-7224
email: vinod.viva@gndel.globalnet.
ems.vsnl.net.in

Southeast Asia (Brunei, Cambodia,
China, Malaysia, Hong Kong, Indonesia,
Laos, Myanmar, the Philippines, Singapore,
Taiwan, and Vietnam)
Hemisphere Publication Services
1 Kallang Pudding Rd. #0403
Golden Wheel Building
Singapore 349316
tel: 65-741-5166
fax: 65-742-9356

**Visit our Web site at:
www.iie.com
E-mail orders to:
orders@iie.com**